Four Chambers

Four Chambers
Emma Adair

This book is a work of fiction

Names, characters, places, dialogues, and incidents are products of the author's imagination or are used fictitiously. Any resemblance to actual events, or persons living or dead is entirely coincidental.

This is the first published edition

First published in 2025 by Adair Gallery
Copyright © Emma Adair 2025
The moral right of the author has been asserted

ALL RIGHTS RESERVED

No part of this book may be reproduced or transmitted in any form or by any means electronic or mechanical including photocopying, recording or by any information storage and retrieval system, without prior permission in writing from the publisher.

The author and publisher have provided this eBook to you for your personal use only. You may not share or make this eBook publicly available in any way.

No Gen AI technology was used to create or edit this story

10 9 8 7 6 5 4 3 2 1

ISBN (Paperback) 978-0-6489399-1-7
ISBN (eBook) 978-0-6489399-0-0

A catalogue record for this book is available from the National Library of Australia

Cover image sahs94 | Adobe Stock
Book design by Beau Lowenstern

Best read with friends

1

Lilian had secured her favourite seat in the front row of Professor Matthews' legal theory class. With six minutes until the end of the lecture, her best friend Jane had begun writing Lilian a note.

A flat palm slammed on the wooden desk, sending vibrations up Jane's arm. As she lurched back, Jane's eyes lifted to meet Professor Matthews' quivering jowls inches from her face.

The note was pegged under the professor's fingertips. Jane tried to slide the note to safety but the paper ripped. Jane panicked and stuffed the incriminating evidence into her bra.

The professor inspected the remaining corner, sans words. After considering Jane's insolence, she slowly outstretched her hand.

"Give me the note, Jane," Professor Matthews hissed as she leant forward. The words chilled the room. Lilian, mortified, elbowed Jane in the ribs.

Jane gave Lilian a wicked grin then sprung to her feet. Startled, her classmates gasped in unison.

"Never! I would rather go to jail," Jane announced in her loudest voice then crossed her arms and glared at the professor.

Lilian and Mieko exchanged a nervous glance.

The professor returned to her lectern.

Since their first day at law school, Jane and Lilian had been inseparable. The professor had hoped Lilian would outgrow her petulant friend but as their education progressed, their devotion to each other remained.

Professor Matthews couldn't resist the curl at the corner of her lips at Jane's audacity in the face of certain failure. What Jane lacked in legal acumen she made up for in flare.

"I have no doubt you would go to jail before giving me that note, Jane, because you are the most stubborn student I have ever taught," the professor declared as she paced in front of the whiteboards. "Alas, it would be remiss of me not to use your predicament to compel our legal minds to reach their fullest potential."

"It's a trap, Babe," Luke called down from the rear of the auditorium and the class giggled.

Now in their final year together, the professor was not concerned about scolding Jane publicly. The students were well acquainted, and relished an intellectual battle.

Jane turned to address her boyfriend and his cronies in the back row. "Luke, this is an excellent opportunity for Professor Matthews to impart more of her exemplary legal wisdom upon us and I would appreciate it if you would show her some more respect."

The room erupted into a chorus of retorts and cheering.

Professor Matthews, amused by Jane's flagrant hypocrisy, hushed the class. "Thank you, Jane. Please stand if you have a legal opinion about the incident you have just witnessed."

Barring Jane and Lilian, the whole class stood.

The professor returned to the lectern to collect a marker then positioned herself at the board.

"Now, mindful we only have two minutes, we will need to move speedily through the different ways Jane has ignited your legal fortitude this apparently boring afternoon."

Primed, they sniggered at the jest and Jane feigned outrage with a sporting smile.

"Please sit down if you are pondering Jane's right not to pay attention in class, as she has paid for this exemplary service of being educated in law." The professor began with the basics, and five sat.

"Please sit down if you are pondering Jane's right to privacy," she added. Three sat.

"Please sit down if your mind turned to your own right to a disruption-free education." She winked at Jane while a further ten sat.

Professor Matthews shrewdly studied the remaining students. "Please sit for anything related to human rights." Six sat.

Seven remained standing.

"Please sit for slander or anything related to proportionality."

Five more students sat, then there were two.

All eyes turned to Luke and Mieko.

Luke grinned supportively at Jane.

Mieko, not expecting to be drawn upon, had gone pale.

"I'm certain I don't want to know what you have to contribute, Luke," the professor quipped. "Mieko, where did you land?"

Mieko mouthed an apology to Jane.

"Jane said she would rather go to jail than give you the note, so maybe she confessed to a crime," Mieko reasoned logically then ruefully dropped to her seat.

The audience oohed in suspense. Jane resembled raspberry jam.

"Thank you, Mieko." The professor, impressed by the breadth of their considerations, wrote 'Jail = Criminal?' on the whiteboard. "Jane, you have thirty seconds."

Jane stood to address her peers, who had heartily enjoyed her roasting.

Lilian pre-emptively leapt to Jane's defence.

"As Jane's lawyer, I have advised my client not to speak lest it impede her defence in court."

Jane giggled. Her classmates booed, dissatisfied.

"Seems you have been saved by the bell, Jane." The professor smiled. "Thank you all for a thought-provoking discussion. Today's lesson is, if you have committed a crime, don't write it on a note in my classroom."

Jane turned to Lilian and whispered, "I think the lesson is, get a good lawyer."

Lilian gathered her belongings and waited at the door while Jane humbly apologised to the professor and promised not to write any more notes.

Once outside, they crossed the quadrangle arm-in-arm and joined the back of the coffee queue.

"In return for your exemplary legal services, I will pay for your coffee," Jane joked.

"Just as well, you can't afford me." Lilian was intrigued, she knew Jane would never create incriminating evidence. "So, what's on the note?"

Jane delved into her shirt, retrieved the paper and handed the message over to its intended recipient.

Lilian burst into laughter, drawing curious looks from students ahead in the line.

"I'm sure Professor Matthews would have been flattered that you think her new haircut makes her look ten years younger."

Jane smiled. Professor Matthews had always been so patient with her. "Maybe, but I didn't want her to feel self-conscious."

2

Lilian leant against the red brick wall of the tiny courtyard. Leaves had blown off the roof and were swirling around her feet while she wrote in her journal.

Lilian was roused from her musing when Lily appeared at the sliding door, draped glamorously in a silk gown.

"Good morning, darling. What time is your exam?" Lily asked then proceeded through the living room to the kitchen.

"Eleven," Lilian called and began to conclude her entry.

Every morning Lily would make them coffee and they would catch up on the previous day. The morning ritual had started after Lilian had moved to Melbourne to live with her grandmother. Lily was out with friends almost every night. If not for their breakfast chat, their paths would rarely cross.

Lily returned with their drinks and sat down opposite Lilian at the tiny white metal table with matching heart shaped chairs.

Lilian shivered and considered the withering green wall. "Almost time to move into the library."

Lilian had transformed the courtyard into a green oasis. But it was nearing the end of autumn and the courtyard had begun to feel chilly. As she did every year, she would shortly shift her journalling inside.

Lily was glad Lilian appeared confident and refreshed. After supporting her through high school and three years of university, Lily was well attuned to her granddaughter's pre-assessment temperament.

"All ready?"

Lilian rebound the notebook and reached for her latte.

"Yes, today is my least-terrifying exam. Two down, two to go."

"Good. Now when will you be finished, so we can get back to planning my seventieth?" Lily enquired impatiently.

"Friday is my last exam. Then one more semester and you will be free of me forever," Lilian teased.

Contrary to Lily's sensationalising, Lilian's schedule had no impact on her entrenched rotation of social commitments.

Lily tutted. "My darling, I want to keep you, it's your pesky exams I want to be rid of."

"That's good, because no one will marry me," Lilian retorted.

Lily rolled her eyes and retreated inside, out of the cold, and away from the conversation.

Lilian's grandfather had died after falling from a ladder and her father had died from a heart attack while walking their dog. Lilian believed, therefore, it was unlikely a potential suitor would be willing to risk their life to marry her. Her family thought she was being ridiculous.

Taunted by a blanket of heavy clouds which had appeared above the courtyard, Lilian cleared her breakfast dishes and put the latest volume of her journal back on the bookshelf above the fireplace.

She threw her toothbrush and toothpaste in her backpack and raced from the terrace through the side streets of Middle Park.

As soon as Lilian boarded the tram to the city the downpour arrived. She settled in the back corner of the carriage, away from the droplets blustering in behind passengers hopping on and off.

Lilian felt prepared. Professor Matthews was an excellent teacher and Lilian had studied meticulously throughout the semester. There was nothing more she could do now, so Lilian relaxed and watched the rain bounce off the umbrellas bobbing past her window.

3

Lilian spotted Jane on the beach, tongs in one hand and bin liners in the other.

Lilian meandered from the carpark at the top of the cliff down haphazard stone steps onto the dunes. She was unimpressed to be celebrating the end of exams by cleaning up rubbish.

Jane was engrossed in an impassioned exchange with the group's leader, Vikram. They usually bonded over recycling. Today, however, the pair were in furious agreement over the appalling decline of the Great Barrier Reef.

Lilian hung back until Jane had finished her rant.

"You're so late. Where have you been?" Jane scolded and thrust a spike at Lilian.

Lilian's servitude of the Wilderness Warriors had been a long-standing bargain. Jane and Luke's relationship had started turbulently. After ten harrowing breakups and the eleventh forgiveness, Lilian had lost her patience. To save their friendship, Jane had offered to never speak of her love life again if Lilian agreed to join the Wilderness Warriors. Lilian accepted and, true to her word, Jane had spared her the heartbreak rollercoaster.

"Sorry. Lily needed me to drop her at the Marina. Her ride cancelled. Another broken hip." Lilian pulled on her gloves and mosquito net hat.

"Oh no, not another one! Not Ruth!" Jane cried, tugging at a chip packet wedged between the reeds.

"No, it was Amber." Lilian picked up a bottle cap.

Jane had met most of Lily's contemporaries at the terrace. Lily's soirees featured unlimited cocktails and then Jane would crawl upstairs to Lilian's bedroom and fall asleep.

"Poor Amber. That's awful. How did your last exam go?" Jane asked, untangling plastic rings from some driftwood.

"Good. I realised afterward that I forgot to include some of the facts in the last question but I'm pretty sure I covered everything else. How about you?" Lilian began picking flakes of plastic from the sand.

"Good. I finished. Now, let's never speak of that class again!" Jane stopped working and gave Lilian an excited squeeze. "I have an idea. But before I ask, you need to promise me you'll sleep on it."

"It makes me so nervous when you look at me like that," Lilian noted warily. "What is it?"

Jane's scheming usually ended up costing Lilian a fortune. Luckily, Jane hadn't gotten them arrested, yet.

"So, as you know, Luke is on tour, and he's missing me, so I said I would go up to Newcastle and see the band, and I want you to come with me," Jane blurted in an increasingly squeaky high pitch.

Lilian felt a pang of sadness. This would likely be the last time they could spontaneously take a trip together. Lilian had applied for the Australian Tax Office graduate program. Jane was dedicated to international law and all her prospective employers were overseas.

Lilian was rostered to work in the bistro at the Marina during their mid-semester break.

"Plane, train or car?"

Jane jumped on Lilian, knocking the half-full bag out of her hand. Cans and bottles spilled out and started rolling towards the ocean.

"We can go whatever way you want. Is that a yes?" Jane squealed excitedly.

The band had only left Melbourne in their mini-van two days ago. With Luke going on tour for the rest of the year, Lilian had assumed Jane and Luke would have broken-up for good this time.

"It's a maybe. I have to check with Doug and get back to you," Lilian qualified as she wriggled free of Jane's embrace and they clamoured after the escaping garbage.

Lilian had worked for Doug at the Marina since she was sixteen. Lily's solution to Lilian's mother's outrage at Lily leaving her teenage daughter alone at home every night was to secure her granddaughter an after-school job.

"Doug will be cool. I can't wait! We're going to have the best time!" Jane screamed, provoking a disparaging grunt from Vikram.

"Work should be fine, but I'll let you know tomorrow," Lilian tempered as she caught Jane's expression and turned to find Vikram glaring at them.

"Yay," Jane whispered hopefully.

While grateful to be ignorant of their current relationship status, Lilian had clearly assumed wrong. Jane and Luke were still together, and she was about to be re-immersed.

4

Lilian scribbled the specials on her clipboard as Brett and Coen talked over each other. Once Coen had explained how he'd infused the vanilla ice cream with eucalyptus, the waiters were dismissed.

Brett and his husband had recently welcomed a baby and to ease the workload Doug had promoted Coen to co-head chef. An arrangement which, like Brett's beautiful daughter, was still teething.

Lilian raced down to Doug's office to catch him before the Marina opened. His door was open and Doug was on the phone trying to arrange a surprise anniversary dinner for his wife, Tracey. Since Tracey had retired, Lilian had been hosting the bistro. Consequently Friday and Saturday nights were marred by long queues while each entering guest requested a play-by-play of Lilian's week. Doug was chuffed. He thought the line made it seem like the Marina was the hottest early dinner sitting in town.

Lilian waited in the doorway while he finished the call.

"You look sunburnt," Doug commented as he hung up.

"Jane made me clean the beach," Lilian explained.

Doug looked confused.

"Because of the environment," she added.

"What can I do for you, Lilian?" Doug tapped the desk.

"Jane wants me to go to Newcastle and I was hoping to see Mum in Sydney before next semester starts," Lilian said fast.

Doug rolled his wheelchair over to the pinboard and checked the roster.

"I'm sure someone will cover for you. Worst case, I can take over the front counter." Doug gave her a supportive wink. "You've worked bloody hard this semester. You've earned yourself a good break. And I appreciate you helping me with the paperwork while Brett was on paternity leave."

Doug rolled back to his desk and pointed to the door, already on to the next task.

"Thanks, Doug." Lilian scurried back to the kitchen.

Brett was busy teaching a new apprentice tricks to peel potatoes so Lilian went to Coen who was preparing fish.

"Can I grab a copy of your menu with the prices please? I need to write the specials on the board."

Coen, absorbed by his task, pointed his chin toward the drawer next to him. Lilian found the sheet and headed to the storeroom to collect the A-frame.

When Lilian returned, Coen had finished filleting and was cleaning up.

"Are you excited to see Will?" Coen asked scrubbing scales from his palms.

Lilian looked perplexed. "Who's Will?"

"Will. Doug's nephew," Coen clarified, not sure if she was joking.

"Oh, you mean William. I've never met him. He'd left to study medicine in Perth before I started at the Marina. Lucky for me, I got his job."

Lilian dunked a chunk of bright yellow chalk in a container of water.

According to Brett, Tracey had organised for William to take over managing the Marina so she and Doug could travel. Tracey knew her husband was so devoted to his team that Doug would never quit, so she had booked them a non-refundable, round-the-world cruise. Doug wasn't thrilled about being lulled into retirement.

"I can't imagine this place without Doug, but then again I couldn't imagine Brett with a baby and he's an amazing Dad, so here's hoping." Coen handed Lilian a cold ginger beer.

Lilian stood back to admire her lettering.

Coen raised his bottle. "To Doug and Tracey."

Lilian clinked the glass with her chalk. "And here's to our new boss!"

5

Lilian lay on a deck chair in the sunroom of her childhood home. Dorothy sat beside her, proofreading Marcus' history assignment.

Although they only spent a few weeks together each year, Lilian felt the distance hadn't impacted her relationship with her mother. They talked almost every day.

Dorothy was wearing a knee length, olive-green dress with white polka dots and gold sandals, ready for a first appointment with a new client. When Lilian's father had died suddenly Dorothy was forced to assume all the financial decision-making for their young family. Having survived her ordeal, Dorothy now specialised in helping women navigate the minefield she'd once had to traverse alone.

Marcus emerged from the side door and raced across the dewy lawn to grab a school shirt from the clothesline. The twins were truly identical. From a distance even Dorothy couldn't tell Marcus and Tim apart.

Lilian noticed her mother considering Marcus peculiarly.

"What?" Lilian asked.

"Nothing. They just look so much like Eric now they're almost adults." Dorothy placed the essay on the side table and took a mouthful of muesli.

Lilian was taken aback. Dorothy never initiated conversations about her late father. When they were children Dorothy would patiently answer their pining questions but never actively encouraged remembering Eric.

"Why are you thinking about Dad?"

"It would have been our thirtieth wedding anniversary today," Dorothy stated with no emotion.

Lilian was unsure what to make of the seemingly offhand comment. "And how do you feel about that?"

Dorothy laughed. "I feel... not a lot."

She turned to Lilian, reached out and took her daughter's hand.

"It's hard for me to talk about him kindly. He was a terrible husband. It's sad but we were all better off without him," Dorothy confessed bluntly, pulling her hand away to take a sip of tea.

Lilian was stunned. She had not given her father much thought since leaving Sydney. In Melbourne she had been blessed with so many people who had taken excellent care of her like Doug, Brett and Lily. The absence of a father was never a void she felt.

Dorothy smiled ashamedly.

"I was planning on telling you all more about him. I didn't want you to grow up believing your loss was greater than it was, but there was no good time to tell you about his failings. None of you seemed to be affected by his absence and, to be honest, I was avoiding having to ruin your assumption that we had been desperately in love."

"You weren't in love? Then why did you get married?" Lilian blurted, confused.

Dorothy tried to answer Lilian's question fairly.

"We were together for years before we got married and decided to have a baby. Before, our lives had been full of adventure and travel and romance, and we were deeply in love then. But a settled life never suited your father. He hated being stuck at home, he felt suffocated by the responsibility, and eventually he forgot he loved me and that we were still the same people."

Lilian felt disorientated.

"He is dead, isn't he? He didn't run off with a younger woman?"

Dorothy looked pityingly at her daughter. She had not planned to have this conversation today, or at all.

"I wouldn't have put it past him. There may be some long-lost siblings in your future," Dorothy scoffed bitterly.

Lilian looked mortified.

"I'm joking, but there might be." Dorothy laughed.

"I have enough siblings as it is." Lilian managed a weak smile, still processing her mother's revelation. Reluctantly she asked, "Did he love us?"

Eric had been consumed with Lilian when she was born, however as their brood grew the continuousness of young children had worn him down. But he had loved them ferociously. That was not an embellishment.

"Yes, he loved you all. He just hated being a parent," Dorothy mustered guilty.

Lilian was relieved and reassured, a little.

"I don't suppose the curse is lifted because Eric was a bad husband?"

Dorothy laughed.

"You're the only one who believes in the curse, so I guess you can dictate its parameters."

Lilian frowned. She hadn't been bothered by Eric's absence before today, but the inversion was nonetheless confronting.

"Please, don't let my opinion of Eric change the few good memories you have of your father. There's no use wondering what might have been, and I wouldn't have changed a thing."

Dorothy stood up to leave for her appointment and kissed her daughter's scrunched forehead. "Let's go to Bondi for lunch when I get back."

"Okay. Good luck," Lilian agreed, feeling unsettled.

Lilian stared at the breakfast dishes. It had been a frantic week trying to organise the last-minute trip, succeeding a hectic semester, and she was too depleted to process this news. So Lilian left the mess and went back to bed.

6

"That's fucked," Jane commiserated.

"Don't swear," Lilian scolded.

"Sorry, but seriously. There are so many questions. Does Dorothy think they would still be together if Eric was alive? Is she glad he died? Did she kill him? Does Ari know? Did she say she would have left him if he hadn't died?" Jane rambled, shocked by Dorothy's duplicity.

Lilian had borrowed her sister's car to drive them up to Newcastle while Ari was holidaying in Hobart. Lilian took one hand off the steering wheel to punch Jane in the arm.

"Of course Mum didn't kill him! As for the rest, I didn't ask. I think she just meant, don't put him on a pedestal because he wasn't perfect."

Lilian tried to focus on the highway and ignore the myriad of emotions Jane was evoking.

"Mum hasn't dated anyone since, so maybe they would still be together." Lilian had always presumed devotion was the reason Dorothy had remained single.

"That you know of! I don't know what's worse, that Dorothy never told you she didn't love your dad, or that you never asked about him. Where are Eric's family? Didn't they ever talk about him when you were growing up?" Jane continued the interrogation, unable to comprehend the development.

"They're in Brisbane. They call and send cards," Lilian justified, feeling defensive.

Lilian's voice quivered. Jane realised too late she'd been too harsh.

"Sorry. I didn't mean to sound judgemental. It's just so… unbelievable." Jane wished she could recant her reaction.

"I'm not upset. You're right, I've never asked Mum about him. We were always happy. I guess I just never really felt like I was missing anything."

They pulled into a beach town for a break.

"Don't be so hard on yourself. You were sixteen when you left Sydney. If you'd stayed, maybe it would have come up sooner. Besides, it seems like Dorothy was deliberately keeping the truth from you. If she wanted you to know about her marriage she would have told you before now."

"Maybe. Either way, I just hope there are no more surprises. She joked that there might be secret halfsiblings." Lilian turned off the engine and shook the tension from her arms. "Let's get some air."

They strolled along the foreshore and poked around some racks outside the seaside shops. Jane found a flask for Luke and Lilian bought a beanie for Brett's baby. Once they'd scoured the strip, they took coffees to the beach and watched the rip churn.

"I know it's been years since I asked, but how are things with Luke?"

Jane raised an amused eyebrow, without response. Lilian never enquired about her relationship.

"What? We're travelling halfway up the east coast to see your boyfriend, who is touring for six months, after which you're going overseas potentially forever. I'm just not sure what we're doing here?"

Jane winced at the crisp summary. She had been avoiding the inevitable.

"We decided to stay together and if either of us finds someone serious, it will just end naturally." Jane's confidence was betrayed by the worry in her voice.

"To clarify, you can both sleep with other people but not break up unless you fall in love with someone else?" Lilian hypothesised, always the lawyer.

"I guess, but less awful than you make it sound," Jane remarked sullenly.

Lilian felt like she was back in First Year.

"Sorry, I'm only trying to understand your situation so I don't say something wrong at the gig."

Lilian was concerned the arrangement was Luke's idea.

"There's no alternative. We don't want to break up and we don't want to compromise on our own plans. Can you think of a better solution?" Jane glanced at her best friend.

Lilian couldn't, so she offered optimism. "It doesn't really matter how you define whether you're in a relationship, it matters if you find your way back to each other."

"You mean like fate?" Jane pleaded, hopefully.

Absolutely not what I meant, Lilian thought.

"Exactly," Lilian lied, remembering vividly how quickly her patience used to evaporate.

"Thank you." A smile returned to Jane's face, and she leant over the empty coffee cups to give Lilian an unsolicited hug.

"Don't tell Vikram we drank from unrecyclable cups. He will kill us," Lilian joked.

Jane gasped and pointed accusingly at Lilian. "So sneaky, I see what you're doing!"

"I asked about Luke first. I would never try to get out of Wilderness Warriors. I love picking up rubbish." Lilian laughed, wishing with the benefit of hindsight she could get out of spending the night with Jane and Luke.

7

Luke stood behind Jane with his hands around her waist to stop her from falling over. Jane twisted within his embrace and began stroking his face.

From the stool opposite Lilian watched Jane sway, curious to see how long it would take for Jane to run out of bourbon fuelled steam.

The gig had been spectacular. Lilian wasn't a fan of Luke's music but he was an excellent performer. Awkwardly, many of the lyrics were about Jane who didn't seem to mind their relationship turmoil being broadcast to strangers.

Lilian was startled by a tap on her shoulder and turned to find Jamie sitting at the table behind.

"Hi, Lilian." Jamie smiled warmly.

"Hi, Jamie. I didn't realise you know Luke," Lilian replied, surprised to see her Debate Club captain in a different state.

"Who's Luke?" Jamie answered, looking perplexed.

"Luke is the band." Lilian pointed across their table at Luke who was now kissing Jane.

"I don't know that guy. I'm in Newcastle for my cousin's wedding tomorrow," Jamie clarified. "So, you're a groupie."

"Absolutely not! Well, maybe. We did follow him up here. Luke and Jane are in my year at uni. Believe it or not, one day they will be lawyers."

Luke began gathering Jane's belongings.

"Where are you staying?" Jamie asked.

"We're in a hotel on the waterfront, just around the corner. Luke and the band have a minivan. Although I'm pretty sure I'm about to be abandoned," Lilian noted, embarrassed by her friends' brazen passion.

"We were just about to leave too. I can walk you back to your hotel," Jamie offered.

"That would be great. I've got to pay our tab. Meet you at the door?" Lilian replied, relieved she wouldn't have to walk back to the room alone.

"Sure, see you out the front."

Lilian turned back to their table. Luke had one arm around Jane and one arm around their bags. Jane's face was pressed against Luke's neck. She had fallen asleep.

"Do you mind if I take her back to the van?" Luke asked sheepishly, mindful Lilian would be on her own.

"I would love it if you could take drunk Jane with you and return sober Jane in the morning." Lilian tied Jane's hair up so she wouldn't choke when she threw up later.

"Thanks, and thanks for coming up to support us. It wouldn't have been the same without our biggest fans." Luke tried unsuccessfully to lift his arm to give Lilian a high five.

"You're welcome, you were amazing. I'm glad I came. See you tomorrow," Lilian admitted and headed to the bar to settle Jane's account.

Lilian wondered as she waited in line whether she technically was a groupie.

Jamie was pacing the pavement by the time Lilian made it outside.

"Thanks for waiting," she apologised, grateful for the company.

They started walking. Lilian led the way to her hotel.

"No problem. I needed to move. We've been sitting all weekend. Who gets married in winter anyway?" Jamie joked.

Lilian laughed. "I'm probably not the right person to ask about weddings. If you want to talk about tax law, that's more my area of expertise."

"Don't get me wrong, I love weddings," Jamie added hastily.

"You love weddings, do you?" Lilian repeated, endeared by his clumsiness.

"I mean, I love weddings as much as women. "He blushed.

"Do you need a shovel?" Lilian teased. She knew Jamie wasn't a misogynist. He'd started a petition to have the wives' names added to the titles of all the buildings on campus named after men.

"Yes, I do." Jamie laughed and swiftly changed the subject. "It's so strange I ran into you. I had been meaning to call you."

"Really, what about?" Lilian was surprised, he'd never called her directly.

"I wanted to ask you whether you would be interested in joining the A-league?"

"What happened to Hirru and Iluka?"

"Iluka quit to focus on his assignments. Hirru thinks there's something else going on but Illuka insists he's just busy. So we need someone to train with us for our next debate at Monash. I was hoping you'd consider filling in?"

Jamie was a brilliant debater. He could speak convincingly about anything. Lilian had once watched him win a debate over whether sandwiches should have crusts. It was one of the most compelling speeches she'd ever heard.

Lilian turned into a side street. "Mukund, Ariel and Rachel are far more experienced. Why would you pass over the B-league team?"

Lilian knew accepting the invitation would be controversial. Mukund had been yearning to break into the A-league for years.

"I want to give Iluka time to reconsider. He's a brilliant First Chair. If I ask any of those three they'll want to stay," Jamie admitted.

Lilian was slightly offended but appreciated Jamie's honesty. She'd always been deterred from the upper echelons because it was uncomfortably competitive. Lilian loved debating in the C-league with Ruan and Kerry where there was no pressure.

"I'd be happy to help against Monash. I'm sure I'd learn a lot," Lilian agreed, already feeling anxious at the thought of performing in front of an auditorium full of raucous rivals.

They arrived at the hotel's entrance. Jamie scanned Lilian from head to toe as he opened the door for her.

"You seem remarkably sober, compared to your friend."

They entered the lobby.

"That's because I don't drink," Lilian explained.

"Interesting, neither do I." Jamie lent down and kissed her cheek, catching the corner of her lips, then whispered in her ear. "Goodnight, can't wait to have you on my team."

8

Lilian could hear music blaring as she opened the front door. She walked down the hallway, past the library, the stairwell, then Lily's bedroom, and emerged in the living room to discover it had been transformed.

There were corkboards propped up against the walls. The couches were covered with swatches, menus, invitations and seating arrangements. And there were shopping bags full of samples strewn across the carpet.

"I'm home," Lilian shouted. She dropped her backpack on the armchair and turned down the volume.

Lily was in the courtyard. She looked up and gave Lilian a broad smile.

Given the recent spate of hip breakings, Lilian was nervous every time she put the key in the front door and was relieved to find her grandmother uninjured.

"Hello, darling." Lily poured Lilian a cup of tea from the teapot.

"What's all this?" Lilian bent down and gave Lily a hug.

"I decided to book the Marina for my party. I would have loved to have had it at the terrace but there have been so many falls in the last year. Doug suggested it would be safer to use the function room. What do you think?"

"Great idea. It won't be as cosy, but you can fit heaps more people," Lilian agreed encouragingly, sipping her tea.

"That's exactly what I thought." Lily looked intensely over her glasses to examine Lilian. She had spoken to Dorothy and had been hoping her granddaughter was all right. "Enough about me, how was your holiday?"

"You spoke to Mum?"

"Yes, darling. I'm sorry she was so curt. It takes two to tango," Lily said irritated.

"What do you mean?" Lilian asked, taken aback by her grandmother's tone.

"Dorothy told me what she blurted out wasn't planned. It sounded to me as though your mother oversimplified a complicated situation."

"Are you saying Dad wasn't as bad as Mum made him out to be?" Lilian was even more confused than she had been after she'd spoken with Dorothy.

"No, they were having a hard time when he died. But like all marriages, I'm sure there would have been good times again," Lily recalled regretfully. "Dorothy and Eric had always been free spirits. They were dysfunctional whenever they had to rely on the other for anything, but it worked for them. If she'd had a husband who wanted to do everything together she would have felt suffocated and been miserable. They just needed more time. Your father wasn't a scoundrel."

Lilian didn't know what to think. Maybe it was easier for her mother to believe their family were better off without Eric because the alternative was too painful. Maybe Lily was wrong and Eric had been a terrible husband.

"I guess I will never know because he died. None of us will ever know what might have happened," Lilian surmised, but the rational reasoning didn't deter the feeling of hopelessness that washed over her.

Lily got up and embraced her granddaughter, and Lilian allowed herself to cry over her father for the first time she could remember.

"I feel ridiculous. I don't even remember him enough to miss him." Lilian sobbed. "Did you know it would have been their thirtieth wedding anniversary?"

As Lilian's tears slowed, Lily returned to her heart chair.

"I did. Grief is a strange companion, it affects us all differently. Russell was the love of my life, and he gave me your mother, but I'm also grateful for so many other things that came after. I don't have any regrets and your mother wouldn't either," Lily said, trying to assure her granddaughter that losing their husbands were not defining moments in their lives.

Lilian wiped away the last of her tears. "Mum and Eric sound like Jane and Luke."

"They were nowhere near as ludicrous." Lily laughed at the comparison. "How was the band? Worth the trip?"

"They were great. Jane decided to stay on the road with Luke for another week."

"Typical Jane." Lily tutted.

"It was fine. I ended up driving back to Sydney with a friend from uni," Lilian commented innocuously.

"Which friend?" Lily asked, noticing Lilian's uncharacteristically vague explanation.

"His name's Jamie. He's the captain of my debating club. Not

Ruan, the whole club." Lilian tried desperately to sound casual.

"So Jamie went to Newcastle without a way to get home? Doesn't sound like a particularly responsible leader," Lily prodded, detecting there was more to the story.

"He was there for a wedding with his family, he just drove back with me instead of them. I'm helping his team while one of their debaters is on leave. We thought it would be a good opportunity to get started on our first debate." Lilian became very aware, under her grandmother's prying gaze, that there was no escape route from the courtyard.

"I see, and what is the debate topic?" Lily asked, charmed by Lilian's bashfulness.

Lily had assumed she'd never met any of Lilian's boyfriends. However given Lilian's reaction to her banal questioning, she realised Jamie may be Lilian's first real crush.

"We don't have the topic yet. We were just talking about general strategies." Lilian blushed. "I have to unpack. I'm meeting the team for practice."

Lilian left the remainder of her tea undrunk and raced inside, ruffling decorations as she hurriedly collected her luggage.

Lily decided not to tempt fate. "Have fun. I'm sure you will be excellent."

9

Lilian had gone to the Marina to study before work and was eating a focaccia Brett had left for her on the kitchen bench. Mid-bite, she was distracted from her reading by a knock on the kitchen doorframe.

Lilian looked up to find a guy wearing boat shoes, caramel slacks and a white polo shirt, clasping a bleeding finger.

"Hi, do you know where I could get a Band-Aid please?" the stranger asked politely.

"Sure, follow me." Lilian snapped into work mode and proceeded to lead him to the first aid room. "It's a bit of a hike."

Lilian cut through the bistro and they walked around to the boardwalk.

They arrived at a small cabin at the top of the jetty and Lilian unlocked the door. "Sorry, we have a first aid kit in the kitchen, but it wouldn't have been very hygienic to fix you up in there."

He followed her into the room and she directed him to the sink.

"No, Doug wouldn't have been very happy with that." He smiled.

Lilian was caught off guard, he wasn't one of their regulars. "Are you a friend?"

Lilian rummaged around in the drawers trying to find the antiseptic.

He turned on the tap to rinse his finger and reached over her head and opened the cupboard where the antibacterial cream was stored.

"Sort of." He laughed. "Do you mind if I take it from here, I'm a doctor."

Lilian realised abruptly why he was grinning.

"William! Sorry, I didn't recognise you. I'll get out of your way." Flustered, Lilian fumbled for the door handle then sprinted back to her lunch.

Lilian stood in the kitchen and watched the second hand click around the clockface. She had panicked, she shouldn't have left William wounded and alone.

Just as Lilian had decided to go back to check on him, William emerged in the doorway.

"Are you alright? Can I get you a drink or some food?" Lilian offered guiltily, embarrassed at abandoning him while injured.

"All good. It was only a little nick from my bike chain." William displayed his professionally bandaged pointer. "Lemonade would be great please."

He entered the kitchen, lent on the counter and examined the titles on her pile of books. "Do you always study at work?"

She passed him a bottle from the drinks fridge. "Not normally. Lily is hosting her party planning committee in the living room."

"I thought Lily is having her seventieth here?" William frowned.

"She is. They basically drink cocktails, talk about Lily, and do no planning at all. It's very noisy."

"Sounds fun," William joked. He had known Lily his whole life. She was a spectacular host.

"They are fun. I am less fun." Lilian laughed in response to William plucking the Constitution of Australia from the middle of the stack.

"I'm sure you're fun when you want to be," William replied intensely and rested his forearms on the counter to inspect the Constitution.

Lilian swooned involuntarily and was grateful he wasn't looking at her to catch her brighten.

"What are you studying?" William asked.

"I'm majoring in tax law." Lilian patted her notes. "But this is for a debate."

"Nice, what's the topic?"

"Whether Australia should become a republic. I'm First Chair. We're affirmative. I'm terrified," Lilian admitted.

William looked up from the page and stared into her. She held his gaze and felt heat creep up her neck.

Lost in William's eyes, Lilian was unaware Brett had returned with a crate overflowing with basil.

"Well, this is unsanitary!" Brett interrupted, alarmed by Lilian's grubby library books strewn across his preparation bench. "I see you have become acquainted with William."

Lilian peeled herself away from the moment to find Brett looking amused and bewildered.

"Hi, Brett, sorry I was catching up on some work over lunch. Thanks for the delicious sandwich!" She stuffed the books into her backpack, then sprayed the surface with sanitiser.

Brett had been feeding Lilian since she'd arrived in Melbourne. In return, Lilian did Brett's paperwork.

Brett placed the basil on his re-sterilised bench and gave

her a hug.

"We missed you. I can't wait to hear about your trip." Brett turned and addressed William coolly as he unpacked the herbs. "Welcome back, I have a lot of ideas for the spring menu. Are you starting next week?"

William straightened up and towered over Brett.

"Thanks. I am, but Doug will be here for a while to train me before they leave for Darwin."

"Great. Well, if you don't mind me asking, how are you feeling about the responsibility, given you no idea how to run a marina? We are all here to help you, of course," Brett queried condescendingly.

William was unphased by the hostility. "I understand your concern, Brett. Having an inexperienced boss is a hassle. I managed a marina in Perth."

"Really, I thought you were studying in Perth," Brett bated sarcastically.

Lilian was shocked by his unprovoked rudeness.

William didn't flinch. "Apologies, Brett. I was unclear. I studied medicine full-time, I worked as a manager of a marina part-time on the weekends, and in my spare time I volunteered giving free medical care to veterans."

William collected his lemonade bottle, locked eyes with Lilian, and gave her a reassuring wink as he exited the kitchen.

"Brett, I have a meeting with Doug. I'm looking forward to hearing your menu ideas," he called from the hallway.

"How arrogant!" Brett complained to Lilian, inflamed by William's composure.

"What was that about? What's wrong with you." Lilian was astonished at her friends' gratuitous shakedown.

"I'm just feeling nervous about an amateur destroying my kitchen," Brett justified unconvincingly. Brett mimicked William bent over the bench, flirting with Lilian. "What was this about?"

"You hypocrite!" Lilian laughed and soaked his apron with sanitiser.

Brett slid off the bench, he needed to start preparing for the dinner sitting. "You can't trust boys that beautiful, Lilian. Now, get out of my kitchen. You are distracting me with all your drama!"

10

Jane had tuned out of Professor Matthews' advanced ethics lecture and was ogling Lilian. Jane hadn't seen Lilian since Newcastle, but she looked more grown up somehow.

Thoroughly disinterested in the prescribed considerations of virtue, Jane reached over to Lilian who was scribbling notes furiously and stroked her face.

"What are you doing?" Lilian hissed. Jane always got bored toward the end of class. Lilian was accustomed to such eccentricities.

Spending her last semester with Lilian was the only reason Jane had come back to Melbourne. Jane hated the thought that their connection was born of convenience but, in truth, they didn't share many common interests outside their affection for each other. They had never had to work at their friendship, class always brought them back together.

"You look different," Jane whispered suspiciously and lent over and sniffed Lilian's hair and then, unsatisfied, started to prod her thigh and bicep.

"Jane, stop poking Lilian," Professor Matthews demanded from the lectern.

Lilian giggled.

"It's not my fault. She looks different. Don't you think so, Professor? Look at her face." Jane stared hard at Lilian's cheek.

Mieko inspected Lilian's other side.

"She looks the same," Mieko reported to Professor Matthews.

Lilian was trying not to laugh.

"Lilian, are you the same?" Professor Matthews sought Lilian's counsel on the accusation.

"I can confirm, Professor Matthews, I'm exactly the same," Lilian managed seriously.

"Jane. First warning." Professor Matthews ended the interlude, clicked through to the last slide of her presentation and seamlessly continued.

"You are not the same," Jane reiterated, undeterred.

Lilian smirked and ignored her.

After class they walked across the quadrangle to their favourite café and Jane filled Lilian in on the rest of her adventure on the road with Luke.

As Jane talked, Lilian's guilt swelled. She hadn't told Jane about Jamie.

Lilian had spoken to Jamie every day since Newcastle. Although they only ever met to discuss the debate, she felt like their collegiality might be something more. He was so attentive, he always wanted to know about her day. But Lilian had known Jamie for years. She didn't want to say anything to Jane yet, in case it turned out he was just being friendly.

Jane was winding herself into an emotional frenzy. Having been absent for the progression, Lilian felt unqualified to offer an opinion on Jane and Luke's current relationship dynamic.

"Jane, you know I'm always here to listen, but I'm not sure what you want from me?" Lilian immediately regretted her choice of words.

"Tell us how you really feel!" Jane spat.

Lilian reached over and took Jane's hand.

"I'm so sorry. I didn't mean that I don't want to help." Lilian stopped and thought about what she really wanted to say. "You know I've never been in love. I've never had to make the decisions you've had to make about your future. But do you want to marry Luke? Do you believe he's the only person that can make you happy?"

Jane was touched by Lilian's effort and considered the question.

"Luke loves me no matter what I do, and he never tries to change me. He never criticises me and he's never bored with me. What could be better than that?" Jane reflected earnestly, with aching hollowness.

Lilian had always thought their mayhem was immature, but now she wondered whether perhaps she had misunderstood their connection.

There was nothing Lilian could add, so she sat with Jane in contemplative silence.

Jane eventually yawned and stretched like she had just gotten out of bed.

"If there is someone else better for me and I'm with Luke, I'll never know. I guess ignorance is bliss," Jane concluded profoundly.

"Professor Matthews would be impressed by your reasoning." Lilian laughed.

Jane's usual airy demeanour returned.

"I love her so much. Do you think I should tell her?" Jane pondered mindlessly.

"No! I'm not sure what happens after the first warning," Lilian quashed, relieved to see her friend smiling again.

11

"Even though we lost, you were great tonight. Do you feel ready for Monash?" Jamie asked Lilian, shaking droplets off his raincoat as they huddled under his umbrella.

"Yes, thanks to you and Hirru. You guys have been amazing," Lilian gushed at his flattery.

Lilian had assumed the rivalry she'd witnessed as an outsider translated to animosity between the teams but had found, behind the scenes, everyone was generous and supportive. At the end of every mock debate Jamie and Hirru would give Lilian tips and strategies to deal with nerves, work on structure and be more convincing. The training schedule was gruelling, but Lilian was improving quickly.

"Iluka might have a fight on his hands if he wants to come back," Jamie hinted.

The tram pulled up and they climbed aboard the empty carriage.

"No way, you practice every night. I'd never get all my assignments done."

"That's a shame. I'll miss you," Jamie said sulkily.

"I'm not dying." Lilian laughed. "I don't know how you make it to training every day. When do you study?"

"In the morning, mostly. I'm usually up at five, then I go

for a run. I make time for the things that matter to me," Jamie said. "Are you a morning person?"

"Not that early! I write in my journal most mornings."

"Oh really, what are you recording?"

"When I started I used to write what I did the day before. Now it's more about things playing on my mind." Lilian felt self-conscious, her explanation hadn't truly captured the ritual's significance.

The tram stopped for passengers at the State Library.

Jamie had been sitting next to her and shifted to the seat opposite so he could see her expression. "What's been on your mind?"

Lilian hesitated, not sure if he really cared or if he was just being polite.

"My father died when I was young and I've been learning more about him recently. I've just been reflecting on whether my perception of him has changed," Lilian confessed, worried she'd been too personal.

"I'm sorry to hear that." Jamie placed his hand on Lilian's knee and squeezed it affectionately.

She was moved by his sincerity. "Thanks, I'm fine. It's just stuff in the background."

Jamie pulled his hand away.

"Running is my outlet. I think through things which are bothering me. The lawyer in me recoils at writing anything down unless it's absolutely necessary." Jamie cringed and they both laughed.

The tram waited at an intersection.

Jamie looked out the window. "This is me. Before I forget,

would you like to come to a house party at my place in a few weeks? Nothing special, just a few mates."

"Sure, that would be great." Lilian blushed, excited for an opportunity to see Jamie again after the end of her A-league secondment.

"Awesome, I'll text you the details." Jamie unclasped his umbrella and braced for the tram to jolt to a stop.

Lilian realised Jamie had missed his train station while they were chatting. "You should have got off at the last stop."

Jamie was charmed by her naivety.

"I know." He leant over and kissed her cheek before he stepped out into the rain.

12

Lilian ran down the hallway and flung open the front door.

William, startled, clutched his chest, mimicking a heart attack. "Hi."

"Hi." Lilian froze. William's beauty was arresting. No matter how many times Lilian saw him, she was always taken aback.

"Did you need me to pick up the party decorations?" William asked awkwardly, worried by her surprise that he may have got the day wrong.

"Sorry, I was just thinking about an assignment. Come on in." Embarrassed, Lilian moved out of the doorway.

William walked toward the living room.

"It's probably been a decade since I was last here." William examined the photos of Lily and family lining the hallway. "None of you?"

"That wall was full well before I got here. There are a couple of me upstairs. I don't take many photos, actually, I don't even think we have a camera?" Lilian stopped herself rambling.

Giant plastic bags were stacked on the couch, ready for transport.

"Just these?" William asked, lifting the packages effortlessly.

"Yes, thanks." Lilian raced up to her room. She could hear William rustling up the hallway.

Lilian grabbed her bag and rushed back down the stairs then locked the front door.

William was waiting in the Marina's work van.

She jumped into the passenger seat. William watched patiently as she fumbled with her seatbelt.

"All good?" William checked.

"Yep, ready to go." Lilian exhaled heavily once the buckle finally clicked into place.

William started the engine and began to drive toward the esplanade.

"You seem a bit anxious. Is the debate worrying you?" William enquired, focused on the road.

"I'm fine. I was researching some tax stuff and lost track of time."

"Tax law major, I remember. How did you get into tax?"

"At uni. I'd always wanted to be a lawyer," Lilian skimped, not wanting to bore him.

"What is it about tax that made you want to specialise?" William persisted, genuinely wanting an answer.

Lilian tried to find the right words. "I guess, because it's pure."

"Intriguing. You're going to have to explain that, sorry, I'm a doctor." William slowed down for a red light.

"Tax law is about equity. Other types of law are about justice. I love what tax represents about us and what we value, and how those values are expressed in the way we measure our contribution to society."

William stared at Lilian, and she felt exposed.

"That's the most eloquent explanation of tax I've ever heard," he replied, enamoured by her passion for her work.

"Why did you study medicine?" Lilian reciprocated, eager to deflect the attention.

"My whole family are doctors, it was written in the stars," William joked, indicating to change lanes.

"Not your whole family. Doug isn't a doctor," Lilian teased.

William laughed. "Actually, Doug is a doctor. Well, he could be a doctor. He has a medical degree but he hated medicine. He changed careers the second he graduated."

"Wow. I've worked with Doug for years. I can't believe he's never mentioned it," Lilian said, affronted by the omission.

"I wouldn't take it personally. I don't think he even remembers." William smiled gently.

"So you really are from a family of doctors. Was there ever anything else you wanted to do?"

She had wanted to be a lawyer in Melbourne from as young as she could remember. She wasn't even sure how she first learnt what a lawyer was.

"Not really. My parents are both in general practice. To be honest, I didn't even know there were other jobs until I was a teenager."

Lilian frowned at the joke.

"It takes a particular mindset to be a doctor which I never had to learn because my parents raised me in their clinic. Doctors from non-medical families tend to struggle at the start."

"I'm not sure what you mean?" Lilian admitted.

William turned off the engine and leaned back in his seat. "When you're treating patients, they've come to you because they need your help. If you aren't used to that, it can feel like every person you see is unhappy and then eventually you get burnt out. It can be depressing if you don't approach your work empathetically. I'm with people in the most intimate moments of their life. Birth, death, heartbreak, fear. It's the most human you can be, it's a real privilege. Medicine shows you what really matters. Like tax."

Lilian was captivated by the weight of his voice, and equally mesmerised by his eyes.

"Shall we go in?" He pointed to the Marina and Lilian realised they were in the carpark.

William jumped out of the van. Lilian composed herself as he unloaded the bags, then they went inside.

He left Lilian for the storeroom, and she went to the kitchen to see what Brett had made for her lunch.

Lilian found a salmon burger and a note saying there was a surprise in the fridge.

Lilian opened the door to the cool room.

Brett had been crafting a bespoke birthday cake for Lily. His latest attempt was waiting on the middle shelf for Lilian's review.

Lilian scooped a dollop of icing from the base.

"Nice cake," William said from the fridge door. "See you later."

"Thanks for the lift."

"No problem. I like spending time with you." William grinned.

Lilian blushed. "Me too."

13

A row of waiters serenaded Lily with a melodic Happy Birthday harmony.

Basking in the glow of her birthday candles, Lily was as radiant as Dorothy could remember.

Lily blew out seven candles, one for each decade, and their amenable attendant took the cake.

"My darlings, thank you for dinner," Lily said to Dorothy and Lilian, getting emotional.

"You're welcome, Mum." Dorothy took Lily's hand, becoming overwhelmed herself.

Dorothy and Lily's relationship had been fractured since Eric died. Lily had taken Dorothy's decision to stay in Sydney personally and resented the time she'd lost with her grandchildren. After Lilian had moved into the terrace their relationship had gradually begun to recover as they worked together to raise her. However, Lily had aged quickly in the past five years. Dorothy hoped Lily still had a few more milestones.

Lilian, mortified, buried her head in her hands while her grandmother flirted with a waiter a third her age as he served her dessert.

Dorothy watched with amusement. Lilian had always been a pensive child, but Dorothy felt living with Lily seemed to have pushed her daughter even further into reservedness.

"I can't tell you how good it feels to be old," Lily said contentedly.

Lilian was perplexed by the statement. "What do you mean?"

"I've had a wonderful life. There's not much more future for me to worry about. Days are more enjoyable when you can live in the moment," Lily explained, savouring the rich flavours.

Lilian laughed. Lily's nonchalance was juxtaposed to her effervescent social life. "You have more plans than anyone I know."

Dorothy felt a pang of envy, their rapport was effortless.

Lily noticed her daughter flinch, recognising the feeling.

"Darling, don't be jealous. Your daughter may live in my house, but I'm not her mother. I'm your mother," Lily said tenderly.

Tears welled in Dorothy's eyes. It was hard for her to gauge from a distance how Lilian had been impacted by their conversation about Eric. In seeking to shield her children from the ugly memories of their father, she had also denied them the moments in which he had proved his adoration. It had been easier to delete Eric from their childhoods than disingenuously cherry pick the good memories while ignoring the bad. But that hadn't been fair, and Dorothy knew she had to make it up to Lilian.

"Sometimes I wish I'd brought the children back to Melbourne," Dorothy shared sadly.

"Are you thinking of moving?" Lilian asked.

The twins were in their final year of high school. Given Lily's age and their decades apart, the distance had been playing on Dorothy's mind. "I assume you aren't planning on living with your grandmother forever?"

Lily interjected.

"Don't you two get any ideas about moving me out of my home. I'm going to die in my library with a cocktail in my hand!"

Lilian had no doubt Lily would never leave the terrace.

"I don't know where I'll end up after uni, but I don't want to leave. I'm happy where I am." Lilian looked forlornly to Lily for reassurance.

"You are welcome to stay as long as you like, darling," Lily confirmed and snuck a wink to Dorothy.

Given the spring in Lilian's step lately, Lily didn't think it would be long until she had a spare bedroom.

14

"This topic is too confronting. I should have stayed on tour with Luke," Jane complained as Lilian and Mieko started Professor Matthews' ethics quiz.

"Seriously, fifty questions is overkill," Mieko agreed, leaving Lilian, as usual, to defend the veracity of their education.

"I think ethics is fascinating. When we're practicing law, we're likely to face these kinds of dilemmas," Lilian responded encouragingly.

"True," Mieko agreed. Lilian's enthusiasm for studying was contagious.

"Professor Matthews can't hear you," Jane teased.

"We have an hour until class, it won't take long if we spilt them up. Jane, you do the first fifteen, I'll do the middle twenty and, Mieko, you do the last fifteen," Lilian suggested, hoping the reduced workload would encourage Jane to try and contribute.

Jane squinted antagonistically at Lilian.

"It's a tad unethical to take more questions for yourself. Would it not be more ethical if we split the questions evenly?" Jane said, plied with coffee and feeling playful.

Lilian wasn't in the mood.

"You're right. What's a third of fifty?" Lilian placed her pen atop the quiz, crossed her arms and glared at Jane.

Jane defiantly pulled out her phone and divided the numbers on the calculator.

"It's sixteen and two thirds. I think it would be more ethical if we all answered sixteen questions each and then flip for the last one," Jane proposed.

"There would be two questions left over," Mieko corrected while completing her allocation.

"In that case, the first person to finish should do the last two," Jane said.

Lilian resisted pointing out that Jane's interference resulted in her needing to complete more questions.

"Excellent idea. I will start at number seventeen," Lilian placated, having reached her limit for Jane's nonsense so early in the morning.

Jane knew better than to push the point and got to work.

Lilian's phone chimed. She looked at the message, smiled, then placed the phone face down on the table.

A minute later the phone buzzed again and vibrated the table. Lilian ignored the disruption.

The third message was too much for Jane, who stopped working and stared at Lilian.

"What do you want, Jane?" Lilian pre-empted, not looking up from the page.

"Are you going to check your messages?"

"No, I'm working."

"What if it's an emergency?" Jane probed, wondering why Lilian was ignoring her phone.

"It's not. Jane, hurry up. We've got to get the quiz finished before class," Lilian deflected busily.

Jane impatiently tapped her pen on the desk.

"Well, this is an ethical dilemma. Should I steal my friend's phone and check her messages because she's denying the seriousness of the situation."

"That's not an ethical dilemma," Mieko commented impartially. Having finished her third, Mieko started on Jane's unanswered quota.

Lilian sighed and, without looking, lifted her phone and showed Jane the screen.

"Well, well, well. Who is Jamie and who is William?" Jane gloated with a smirk.

Lilian flushed rosily and consulted her phone. She had been expecting messages from Hirru about the debate location.

"It is quite possible there may be an emergency," Jane announced triumphantly to Mieko.

Mieko giggled.

Lilian rolled her eyes and checked the messages. William and Jamie were each wishing her good luck for the debate.

"There is no emergency," Lilian confirmed. She turned off her phone and returned to the quiz.

"Are you kidding!" Jane cried, throwing her hands in the air. "Who are William and Jamie? Who? Who!"

"Jane, you know Jamie is from debating and William works at the Marina," Lilian replied, refusing to acknowledge the unusualness of the contact.

"Oh, I know who they are, but who are they to you?"

Lilian wondered why Jane was so hyperactive this morning. She looked to Mieko for sympathy.

"Are you going to be like this all day? It's my debate tonight,

I need to conserve my energy for an actual argument."

"Okay. I'll let it go today. But, you know, I'm here every day," Jane yielded.

Lilian had finished her questions. "I need to check something at the library. I'll meet you in class."

Lilian fled the study group before Jane could respond. She needed space to think. Lilian had been spending time with Jamie and William, and she had developed feelings for them both. She had promised her journal that she would confront her own ethical dilemma after the debate.

15

Lilian skipped towards Jamie's car.

"I'm jealous of your first-debate high," Jamie joked.

Lilian had gripped the sides of her chair so hard her knuckles had turned white. However, once the adjudicator had called Lilian's name, her apprehension dissipated and she had delivered her speech flawlessly.

"I feel completely invigorated." Lilian beamed, reliving the roar of the packed auditorium when they won.

"Changing your mind about staying on our team?" Jamie enquired with a grin.

The gruelling training had paid off. Lilian had been engaging and convincing. Jamie had been mesmerised.

"One night in the limelight is enough for me. Iluka can have his job back," Lilian insisted, thankful for the experience but mindful of the many commitments she had neglected the past few weeks.

Jamie opened the passenger side door for her. "Iluka will be glad to hear that. He confessed he was bored studying and missed training."

"Thank goodness." Lilian collapsed onto the seat. "I'm never going to get to sleep."

"Do you have class early tomorrow?" Jamie asked, concerned.

"I'll be fine, I'm used to late nights working at the Marina. Although I'm usually exhausted when I get home, not energetic," Lilian acknowledged as they pulled out of the carpark.

"It's a shame neither of us drink or we could go to a bar to celebrate your sensational debut," Jamie ruminated, unable to contrive a legitimate reason not to take her straight home.

"Wow, you remembered. Newcastle feels like a long time ago," Lilian said, amazed Jamie recalled that conversation.

"Believe it or not, I listen intently to everything you say," Jamie teased. "I think we arrived at your hotel before I could ask you why?"

Lilian was flattered.

"I used to get anxiety when I moved here from Sydney to live with my grandmother and alcohol made it worse. I also don't really like the taste. Not drinking has probably saved me thousands compared to some of my friends who seem to spend all their money in pubs. What about you?"

"I'm too busy for a hangover. I find it hard to get up and run if I've drunk the night before. I was surprised that I don't miss it."

Lilian's elation was morphing into jitters.

"In that case, I'll have to take you and Hirru out for dinner to thank you for helping me prepare."

"That's really sweet. But you may want to also invite the B-league team. Outside debating, Hirru and I have nothing in common. You'll see when you come to my party."

"How so?" Lilian was intrigued. Hirru was delightful. It was hard to imagine the three of them wouldn't be able to find something to talk about for a couple of hours.

"The debaters find my other friends," Jamie paused to choose the right word, "tedious."

"Are your other friends tedious?" Lilian wondered, trusting of Hirru's judgement.

Jamie laughed affectionately. "I have a lot of friends. Some groups are incompatible. Not in a bad way, they're just different."

"Well, I look forward to meeting all of your friends," Lilian replied open-mindedly, unsure whether she wanted to participate in a socially awkward gathering.

"I didn't realise you're not from Melbourne," Jamie remarked.

"It's strange to hear you say it that way. I was sixteen when I moved here but I consider Melbourne home."

"Sorry, I didn't mean to offend you," Jamie apologised, worried he'd been rude.

"That's okay. I'm not offended. I never really felt like Sydney was home. My mother was homesick for Melbourne my whole childhood. I think I got it in my head this was where we were meant to be."

Lilian had always told everyone she wanted to go to Melbourne to study law, but the decision was more personal.

"No wonder you were anxious, moving to a strange city on your own as a teenager must have been hard." Jamie was impressed by her strength. "Do you think you'll move back to Sydney after you graduate?"

"I don't mind going back for a graduate position," Lilian supposed.

Jamie didn't comment. He appeared miserable for someone who had just won a prestigious debate.

The adrenaline had drained away and exhaustion had hit.

Lilian didn't have the energy to reignite the conversation and they sat in silence for the rest of trip.

"Left turn at the end of the boulevard."

Lilian was suddenly aware she wouldn't see Jamie again until the party.

"The terrace is just here."

Jamie manoeuvred into a neighbouring driveway and switched off the engine. "I had a great time with you. I mean, I've had a great time getting to know you, and, I was wondering if you would like to have dinner with me sometime?"

Jamie blushed.

"I love going out for dinner. There are heaps of good restaurants in St Kilda," Lilian said casually, then opened the car door and stepped out onto the pavement.

"I'm asking you on a date," Jamie added, concerned Lilian had missed the subtext.

Lilian didn't want to say goodnight, but she had to go to sleep. She had Professor Matthews first thing in the morning.

Lilian smiled, she'd never seen him nervous. "I know, I'm saying yes."

16

Jane was in her element hosting Lily's sparkle themed seventieth birthday celebration. Resplendent in a cascading tassel dress and glitter paint, Jane called Dorothy to the stage.

Dorothy made her way to the lectern, printed notes in hand, gown glimmering under the lights.

Doug had rented a sequined throne and Lily reigned proudly over her subjects.

"Mum, tonight I want to pay tribute to the inspiration you have been in my life and thank you for supporting me through the tragedies we have faced and taking care of Lilian. I miss you every day. In my darkest moments yours is the voice I hear telling me to get up and keep going and not take life so seriously, to appreciate the bad with the good."

Overcome, Dorothy disregarded the speech she'd prepared and addressed Lily from her heart.

"So often I've felt guilty for the distance between us. You in Melbourne, while the kids and I were in Sydney. However, tonight I look around this sparkly room and realise you weren't alone."

A tear rolled down Dorothy's cheek.

"I know you will be missing Russell tonight. My father and the love of your life. Of all your enviable qualities as my friend, your greatest gift as my mother was refusing to let me feel pity for our loss. You taught me the precariousness of life and the importance of celebrating the time we did have and cherishing those memories. You have spent your whole life taking care of people, and bringing joy to their lives, and tonight shows how much you mean to all of us. I love you, Mum. Happy Birthday."

Dorothy walked over to Lily who reached up and cupped her daughter's face. Dorothy lent over and kissed her mother on both cheeks.

"Not a dry eye in the house. Give it up for Dorothy!" Jane bellowed to a rousing cheer. "That was our last speech. Would the birthday girl like to say anything?"

Lily stretched out her hand and Jane passed her the microphone.

"I will stay in my throne, if you all don't mind. I have had a few too many cocktails for these shoes at this age," Lily began, and the guests laughed.

"My darling daughter, so rarely we talk about Russell these days. Even so, some mornings I wake and stretch my arm out to reach for him and I'm still surprised when he isn't there. But I look around the room tonight and can't deny it's hard to feel now, at seventy, that my life has been anything other than spectacular." Lily sighed graciously. "My wonderful family and friends, I love you enormously, thank you for sticking with me this far."

Lily raised the cocktail Coen had designed in her name.

Family and friends clinked their glasses and cheered in her honour.

Lilian was overwhelmed with love for her grandmother and saddened that Lily still pined for her late husband.

Brett wheeled out the final iteration of his culinarily masterpiece.

Jane helped Lily down the steps, accompanied by a chorus of Happy Birthday.

Lily delegated extinguishing her seventy candles to Marcus and Tim.

Dorothy took her mother's elbow and helped Lily back to her seat at the head of the dining table.

Lily and Dorothy sat arm in arm. Lilian watched them talk and realised how much she didn't know about their relationship. It felt like they were resolving a rift Lilian hadn't even known had existed.

The band started their first set. Lilian took photos of Lily and Dorothy and sent them to Ari who was travelling overseas.

Half the guests had started dancing and the other half had formed a line and were waiting for cake.

Lilian was in a daze when William came over and disrupted her thoughts.

"Great speech." He had caught the end of the celebration.

"Mum was amazing. Thanks for covering for Doug so he could come to the party." Lilian looked nervously toward the dancefloor.

"No problem. I'm done for the night. What did I miss?"

"Ruth and Doug spoke first, their speeches were beautiful. The twins wrote a song about Lily, and I recited a poem from Ari."

"Nice. Would you like to dance?"

"I'm not very good," Lilian claimed shyly.

"She would love to dance with you, William," Lily interjected and gave Lilian a non-negotiable glare.

"Sure, why not, other than being a terrible dancer," Lilian said under her breath, then followed William to the dancefloor.

William wrapped his arms around her waist. "No one dances because they're good. They dance because it's fun."

17

Vikram stomped away, defeated in his latest attempt to expose Lilian as an imposter.

"Seriously, what's up with him today? I'm here, picking up rubbish, does it matter why?" Lilian complained while standing in the creek plucking trash off the bank.

"You know Vikram works in mysterious ways. Who are we to question whether you would do a better job if you hadn't been coerced," Jane joked. "It's not you. His girlfriend broke up with him for being too soft on climate change."

"Poor Vikram. He's just trying to win back his lost love," Lilian cooed, Vikram forgiven.

"Speaking of love, you and William were looking cosy last night," Jane crowbarred.

Lilian had been waiting for this comment all morning. "We were just dancing."

"But were you though? Because his hands and feet weren't moving, and your hands and feet weren't moving. Which, I'm pretty sure is hugging," Jane exaggerated.

"Interesting analysis of two people dancing to a slow song surrounded by other people doing the exact same thing. Including you by the way," Lilian retorted. Jane had been spy-dancing with Brett.

"Why are you denying you like William? You're single. He's hot." Jane feared Lilian was oblivious to their explosive chemistry.

Lilian tugged at a plastic bag caught under a rock.

"I'm not denying I like him," she sighed. "I'm just… conflicted. Jamie asked me out after the debate."

"That's so exciting. I assume you said yes?" Jane had stopped working.

"I did," Lilian confirmed.

"Okay, I see the problem. So who will you choose?"

"William hasn't asked me out, so I'll worry about that if he does," Lilian reasoned.

"That's absurd!" Jane was astounded Lilian wasn't more invested in her own love life. "Who do you like more?"

"I don't know either of them very well yet," Lilian replied cagily.

"So you're just going to date Jamie because he asked and if William doesn't ask then you won't have to make a decision." Jane wasn't going to let Lilian off the hook. "If you like them both equally, then ask William out, and try and figure out who would be a better boyfriend."

"Assuming I want a boyfriend," Lilian refuted.

"Stop deflecting!" Jane snapped, annoyed at Lilian's refusal to have a meaningful conversation.

"Sorry, you're right. I like them both and I don't want to choose yet. It hadn't occurred to me to ask William out," Lilian admitted, absorbing Jane's prudent counsel.

The rest of the Wilderness Warriors had disappeared around the creek bend.

"I know you're taking this really seriously," Jane noted, amused. Anyone else would be overjoyed to have two gorgeous guys crushing on them.

"Yes, I'm taking this seriously. What are you implying, Jane?" Lilian asked, unsure of Jane's point. Dating was obviously serious.

"Once I was complaining that I had met Luke too soon and was annoyed because I wanted to have some fun dating. Your response was, why would I date anyone for fun when the purpose of dating is to find someone to marry. So, I assume you think you might marry one of them."

"Did you read my journal?" Lilian eyed Jane suspiciously.

"No! I just know you." Jane laughed. "The fact you're not more invested in the outcome is worrying. If you really think one of them could be it for you, why are you being so submissive?"

"I can't believe you just called me submissive!" Lilian exploded.

"That's exactly what you're being, Miss I'll-just-marry-the-first-guy-that-asks," Jane mocked.

Alerted to their absence by their raised voices, Vikram appeared at the turn, visibly frustrated by their leisurely pace.

"Sorry! We're going as fast as we can," Jane yelled, mindful of his tetchiness, then turned back to Lilian to continue the argument.

Lilian knew Jane was right. "I accept I could be more assertive. With the debate, then Lily's party, and Mum being here, I just hadn't thought about it. So, thank you, you have made a compelling case. It's clear what I have to do now."

"What's that? I'm just never sure with you," Jane joked, hoping Lilian had received the intended message.

"I have to ask William on a date. Then if he says no, I don't have to worry about being a submissive participant in my own destiny."

"That's my girl! You should ask him out because you like him, but I'll take whatever gets you there. Should we have a strategy session?" Jane offered, relieved Lilian wasn't going to ignore her feelings for William.

"That's okay. But thanks anyway." Lilian plucked a bottle from a bush. "How're things with Luke?"

"Don't ask!"

18

Lilian stood under the entrance archway. Jamie hadn't mentioned he lived in a miniature castle.

As she approached to ring the doorbell, the domineering wooden door flung open.

"They're out the back, next to the tennis court," Jamie's sister said. She ushered Lilian inside along with a group who had emerged behind her.

Lilian let them pass then followed them down a hallway, admiring the grand paintings and glass casings filled with ornaments and trophies. Jamie's family were clearly accomplished.

She entered an empty living room. Through its windows Lilian could see people mingling on a tennis court around a makeshift bar decked with fairy lights. She panned the crowd searching for familiar faces.

Lilian spotted Rachel at the end of the patio. The debaters were sitting around a picnic table drinking keg beer.

Lilian manoeuvred around the huddles and slid onto the bench beside Iluka.

Hirru and Mukund, oblivious to her arrival, were locked in an intense discussion.

"Hello, welcome to the nerd's corner," Iluka said, offering Lilian a beer.

"Hi, I don't drink, but thanks. How is everyone?" Lilian asked, overwhelmed.

"Good, Hirru and Mukund are fighting about free speech. I tuned out after about five seconds. Congratulations on your win against Monash. Hirru says you were almost as good as me," Iluka teased with a friendly jibe.

"Thanks, it was a great experience. I was definitely not as good as you. Are you happy to be back on the team?"

"I am," Iluka replied gratefully. "Last semester I fell behind on my reading and it showed in my grades. I've been able to get back on top of things, thanks to you."

Lilian nodded, only half listening, distracted by Rachel death-staring her from the other end of the table. Lilian wondered whether Rachel had heard about the impending date. Maybe Jamie had been telling people? The only person she had told was Jane who wasn't a gossip.

Lilian panned the crowd again but couldn't see Jamie.

"Are you looking for Jamie?" Iluka inquired, breaking her concentration. "We usually only see him for a couple of minutes."

Acknowledging the futility, Lilian turned back to the table. "What's the party for?"

"Jamie does this every semester. I'm not sure why. I think just because he can." Iluka laughed, content that the affluent have parties for no reason.

"I was a little shocked by the mansion," Lilian admitted. The block was ten times the width of Lily's terrace.

"Me too my first time. Jamie doesn't seem like a mansion kind of guy. I think his parents are famous for discovering something in engineering, maybe science? You know, we really don't talk much, given how much we talk," Iluka joked.

"Do you know anyone else here?" Lilian wondered, feeling intimidated by a trendy-looking cluster nearby.

"Just people from uni. Usually Jamie invites friends from high school, and his law firm, some from his football team, and there are a bunch of his sisters' friends here and I think some cousins," Iluka confirmed, confident he'd covered everyone. "Oh, and us!"

"You know a lot about his friends for two people who don't talk." Lilian laughed.

"I've met a few of them over the years. We tend to stick to our groups these days. Hirru and Rachel get here early to claim our table," Iluka explained, inducting her into their survival strategy. Iluka winked. "Although, I think Rachel probably has other motivations. She was not impressed when she heard Jamie had asked you out."

"I thought she looked angry at me," Lilian concurred, unsure how to deal with the situation. She really didn't want to get involved in whatever was going on there.

"Don't worry about it. Jamie would have asked Rachel out if he liked her. He's not shy!"

"Do you mind if I ask how everyone knows?"

"Jamie and Mukund were talking about good date restaurants at training. I assumed it wasn't a secret. Is it a secret?" Iluka asked nervously.

"No, I was just surprised that's all. It's totally fine," Lilian said, uncomfortable, but she couldn't pinpoint why. Surely dating was private, but it wasn't a secret. Lilian felt out of her depth. Dating, thus far, definitely wasn't fun.

19

Staff had assembled in the kitchen for Doug's farewell. Brett had wanted to throw him a leaving party but Doug had refused, so his team had chipped in and bought him a gift. Doug, emotion brimming, had excused himself before anyone could make a speech.

Lilian finished her cupcake then left the gathering to find her boss before they opened the doors for dinner.

William was sitting at Doug's computer.

Lilian poked her head around the doorframe. "Hi. Doug wanted to see me?"

"Hey, do you want to come in and wait? I'm just learning the accounting software," William replied, not looking up from the screen.

"Thanks. Are you okay? You look a little annoyed." Lilian hadn't seen William stressed, he looked quite different when he was scowling.

"I'm not annoyed. This is what everyone looks like when they're doing accounting." William instantly reverted to his usual enigmatic grin. "Except people like you, who love tax."

"I don't love bookkeeping, I'm studying tax law," Lilian corrected and sat down in the chair opposite him.

"The fact that you know the difference is evidence you love tax." William laughed.

"I do love tax," Lilian agreed. "Are you all set for your first day tomorrow?"

William closed the laptop. "Other than trying to remember how to use that software, yes. My stuff is arriving from Perth on the weekend and then I'll be able to wear something other than the same two shirts."

Lilian hadn't noticed. "You don't think you'll go back?"

"No, I missed my family the whole time. My placement is in Bendigo, but I'll be living with my parents until then."

Doug walked in, interrupting their conversation, and sat on his desk. He'd switched to his prosthetic to get fit.

"Lilian, I have been looking for you everywhere. Never mind, I wanted to have a quick chat. Brett's been giving William a hard time and I don't know why. I don't want to leave without making sure my manager and head chef are going to be able to work together. Has he said anything to you?"

Lilian almost gasped, stunned Doug would ask her so bluntly to betray her friend. "I'm not aware of any problems."

William interjected forcefully. "Doug, don't put Lilian in that position. Brett and I are adults. Whatever his problem is, we will work it out."

Doug reddened but continued. "I'm sorry to ask but I'm really worried. You know what Brett's like when he digs into a grudge. I've lost great people over the years because he decided he didn't like them and made everything difficult for them. This time I won't be here to to stop him."

Doug sounded distressed. Lilian had heard the rumours after people left. However, she had only ever been on Brett's good side.

"Doug, this is completely inappropriate. If Brett is bullying staff, I will fire him. This isn't Lilian's responsibility, and you should know better." William snapped angrily, now standing with his hands on his hips.

Lilian was feeling half relieved that William had stood up for her and half insulted that he had spoken for her.

"You're right. I know you're an excellent manager. I will leave it with you to sort it out with Brett yourself," Doug said to William then turned to Lilian. "We'll drop the terrace by on Saturday. Tracey wants to say goodbye to Lily before we leave."

Doug fled the office.

William sat back down at the desk and his composure returned. Lilian stared at him inquisitively, still deciding whether to be offended or pleased.

"Sorry to speak over you. Doug consulting you about another staff member is unethical, especially given you're not involved. It won't happen again, I'm more in tune with legislative requirements," William promised.

Lilian wasn't sure what to make of the comment.

"So, are you my boss now or are you my boss from tomorrow onward?"

"Technically, I start tomorrow. Are you implying I didn't have the authority to chastise my uncle?" William inquired, confused by the question.

"I was going to ask you if you wanted to go on a date, but it sounds like you may find that to be inappropriate if you were my boss, technically?"

"Are you asking me out or are you asking me if you are allowed to ask me out after tomorrow?" William said, amused by her timing.

"I don't know. I guess it depends if I'm allowed to ask you out after tomorrow because, if not, I should probably ask you out today. What do you think?"

"I think I would like to go on a date with you. And you're right, it would be inappropriate for me to ask you out, so thank you for asking, because I wouldn't have." William matched her intensity and waited as she digested his response.

"This is really awkward." Lilian laughed.

William walked around the desk and grazed Lilian's burning cheek. "I would love to keep talking about our date, but I need to open the front door because there's a line of pensioners standing in the rain."

20

Lilian was glad to have recommenced her journaling in the courtyard. The creepers were abloom with fragrant flowers competing with the salty sea air. Yet despite the serenity, Lilian was feeling irritable.

Lily popped her head around the sliding door, saving Lilian from herself.

"Morning, darling. I feel like a chai. Cappuccino for you?" Lily asked, admiring a new rose which had opened overnight.

"Yes please," Lilian replied, finishing the paragraph.

Lily prepared their beverages and came back with a light blanket.

"It's lovely to be back in the courtyard. Aren't I lucky I have you to take care of the awful gardening."

Lilian closed her journal and smiled hollowly at the jest.

"Darling, you look tired and you just woke up. Are you feeling alright?" Lily asked, noticing Lilian's depleted complexion.

"I'm fine, I didn't sleep well, my head is full of racing thoughts," Lilian said, sounding exhausted.

"Thoughts like what? A problem shared is a problem halved."

"No problems, just lots of decisions to make and imperfect criteria," Lilian deflected. "I'm going down to the beach for a walk after breakfast. I'm sure I'll feel better afterward."

"Decisions like?"

"What job will I have? Where will I live? What will my grades be?" Lilian paused and took a giant breath before continuing. "Should I choose Jamie or William? What if they break up with me? What if I choose the wrong one. I just don't know where to start!"

Lilian slumped against the back of her heart shaped chair.

Lily felt disappointed that Lilian wasn't excited by multiple romantic prospects. But knowing her granddaughter, Lily suggesting Lilian lighten up would not be helpful.

"Instead of worrying about things you can't control, why don't you develop your own criteria to help you decide between Jamie and William," Lily suggested, sipping her spiced latte.

As a love novice, Lilian had assumed she would just know which one she liked more. She made a mental note to ask Jane for her advice.

Eventually Lilian smiled. "How do I choose?"

"Darling, it might help you to think about what kind of life you want, so you can gauge which candidate is likely to want the same things."

"It sounds so clinical. I thought I would just fall in love," Lilian said sadly.

"That would be ideal, but just in case, have a think about what will make you happy in the long term. Even if you're not ready to make a commitment, you will have thought about it."

Their homelife was usually light and casual but Lily was always prepared to be parental when needed.

"I'm meeting Ruth for an art gallery tour this morning. Would you like to join us?" Lily asked, reluctant to leave Lilian angst ridden.

Equipped with a strategy, Lilian's disillusion mellowed. "No thanks, I'll just stay here and think about the rest of my life."

21

"As much as I'm enjoying this interrogation, let me just test what I think's going on here," Jamie interjected, putting his hands in the air as though Lilian was pointing a gun at him.

"I'm sorry?" Lilian replied, surprised.

Moonlight reflected off the lake and soft candlelight flickered in the warm spring breeze. Below their table, water gently lapped at the boardwalk.

"I'm a lawyer. You're asking me indirect questions because you're trying to figure something out," Jamie guessed.

At first, Jamie had thought Lilian was nervous. Then he had thought she was upset with him. He hoped he'd finally deciphered why she was so uncomfortable.

Lilian was disconcerted by the accusation.

"It feels like you're trying to figure out whether I'm dating you for fun or dating you seriously," Jamie posed.

"I'm just…" Lilian started to respond.

"Let me finish, please," Jamie interrupted.

"Sorry, go ahead." Lilian was perturbed but interested to hear his justification.

"My parents have an extraordinary marriage. They are best friends, they do everything together and they are infatuated with each other. They stay that way because of the time and effort they spend prioritising their marriage. I would like to think I therefore know what it takes to be a good husband."

Lilian had no idea where the monologue was headed but Jamie was, as always, captivating.

"I'm not afraid of commitment. I don't think marriage is a trap and fidelity doesn't scare me. I'm sure other guys believe having a wife will ruin their lives, but I can assure you I know having a wife who is the right woman for you is probably the best thing that can happen to any man." Jamie paused to draw breath.

"I'm not prepared for a proposal tonight." Lilian laughed nervously.

Waiters hovered quietly in the background, clearing dishes, packing up tables, taking last orders.

"Really, because you asked how many children I want," Jamie retorted defensively. "All I'm saying is, you don't have to ask me all these hypothetical questions. Just ask me what you really want to know."

"I really wanted to know if you want to have children," Lilian teased.

"And I really want to have four children, but it's your body, we can have one or ten if you want," Jamie joked and stretched his hand out, hoping Lilian would take it. "I like you. I'm not looking for a wife tonight, but I wouldn't be here if I couldn't see a future with you."

Lilian was trying not to laugh, he was so articulate. It was a ludicrous conversation.

"I feel the same way." Lilian lent in and took his waiting hand.

"Good! Well, I'm glad that's sorted." Jamie let out an exaggerated sigh.

Lilian was impressed by his honesty and determination to ensure they were understanding each other. All qualities, she realised, that were probably more important than the arbitrary criteria she'd compiled. Lilian felt guilty for the confusion she'd caused trying to ascertain whether they would be compatible.

"Thank you and I'm sorry. Listening to you describe your parents' marriage makes me think you're going to be a way better partner than me," Lilian admitted fortuitously.

Jamie tenderly brushed his thumb over her knuckles. "Why? Because Eric died when you were young?"

Lilian panicked, worried it was too early for Jamie to discover the curse.

"Not just that. My grandfather, Lily's husband, also died young. And my father's side of the family all live in Brisbane. So, I've had no good relationship role models," Lilian realised, embarrassed by her irregular upbringing.

"Then you've also had no bad relationship role models," Jamie countered supportively.

He appeared not to have registered that men die around the women in Lilian's family.

"That's a generous conclusion," Lilian accepted his optimism sadly.

"I believe marriage is hard work. It's two people making the decision they want to build a future together. What happened in other people's lives isn't a relevant consideration for me," Jamie said reassuringly.

In spite of being hypnotically convincing, Lilian believed Jamie meant what he said. Lilian watched him gazing at her adoringly and for the first time felt like she might want to fall in love.

22

Lilian sat in the front row chatting to Mieko about their group assignment.

Professor Matthews started the lecture.

"Where's Jane?" Mieko whispered.

"Don't know." Lilian shrugged.

Lilian messaged Jane but she didn't reply.

Throughout the lecture Lilian checked her phone every few minutes but there was no response. She began to worry. Unlike Lilian, Jane was an incessant messenger.

Professor Matthews shortened the lecture so the groups could work on their presentations.

The professor waved at Lilian, indicating for her to approach the lectern.

"Is Jane all right?" the professor asked.

"I haven't heard from her today," Lilian said, puzzled. Students missed class all the time, professors didn't usually notice.

Professor Matthews pointed to a document open on her laptop. It was an assignment deadline extension form. Jane had written the reason for the request was that her heart had been smashed into a billion pieces.

"The melodrama that is Luke and Jane doesn't usually manifest itself in my paperwork."

Lilian had thought they were both busy finishing assignments. "I haven't spoken to her today. I'll see if I can get through."

Lilian went back to her seat and called. Jane didn't answer.

Lilian tried not to catastrophise.

"She's not answering. Do you mind if I leave now to check on her?"

"Please do. If I don't hear from you, I'll assume Jane's heart is still beating. I'll see you both in the tutorial."

Lilian updated Mieko then detoured to Lygon Street to pick up some of Jane's favourite snacks in case she needed to coax her to open the door.

After an impatient tram ride, Lilian arrived at the apartment building hoping Jane would answer the intercom as she didn't have a backup plan.

"Who is it?" Jane answered croakily.

"Lilian. I have snacks," Lilian replied affectionately.

"What good are snacks if you're dead inside!" Jane moaned theatrically.

Lilian relaxed. Jane was only this ridiculous when she was functioning.

"Jane, open the door!" Lilian yelled.

The lock clicked open, and Lilian took the elevator to Jane's studio on the sixth floor.

The door was ajar, Lilian entered.

Jane was in a ball on the couch.

"Professor Matthews sent me to check on you." Lilian sat next to Jane and began stroking her hair. "What happened?"

"Luke broke up with me, for real this time," Jane sulked.

"Are you sure? Why for real this time?" Lilian asked sceptically.

"He met some girl in Cairns. She joined his band and they're moving to California."

"So what if Luke's new girlfriend cheats on him next week, and he has no money so he can't fly to California, then he comes back to Melbourne and wants you back?" Lilian proposed a far more probable scenario than Luke's whimsical tangent.

"Are you asking if I would take him back?" Jane sat up and greeted Lilian properly with a hug.

"You're the one who called me submissive. Is it over because you've decided to move on, or are you going to take him back whenever his fantasy falls apart?"

Lilian knew she was teetering on harsh.

Jane thought about it.

"I'm too raw. I want to move on but I'm just… shocked." Jane choked back tears, sickened by the thought of Luke with someone else.

"I'm sorry." Lilian pulled the snacks out her bag.

"Thanks." Jane unwrapped a truffle. "It's just so humiliating, he clearly never loved me."

"Luke loves you. He's been adamant from the start he wasn't ready for commitment."

Lilian could see Jane's pain was excruciating but Luke had always dreamt of the touring life, not just the music. Neither could say this was unexpected.

"How would you like to stay at my place tonight? Amber's coming over for dinner and Lily will make you some cocktails and we can cheer you up," Lilian offered, not wanting Jane to mull around stewing on her own.

"Will Ruth be there?" Jane asked hopefully.

"I'm not sure. Let me ask Lily if we can invite her." Lilian was wary this was fast becoming a house party on a school night.

"I'll have a shower and get ready." Jane sprang off the couch excitedly and went into her bedroom to pack.

Lilian made arrangements with Lily for two extra dinner guests.

Jane emerged, duffle packed, uncharacteristically clad in black.

"I'm in mourning," she explained. "Let's go!"

Lilian laughed and hugged Jane then collected the remaining snacks to take back to the terrace.

Jane turned off the lights and locked her door. "Thank you for coming over, I'm so lucky to have you."

"Any time. You should let Professor Matthews know you're alright. She was worried about you."

"She can't have been that worried about me, she refused my extension request," Jane refuted as they got into the lift. "I'll finish my assignment after dinner."

Lilian wasn't surprised. Professor Matthews didn't give extensions unless you were on the verge of death, with a medical certificate to prove it. "Oh really, what did she say?"

Jane laughed. "She told me to buy some glue."

23

Lilian waited nervously on William's porch. She was relieved to find he lived in a normal sized house.

William answered wearing a butcher's apron covered in flour.

"Come in, I won't give you a hug." He grinned and leant over to kiss her cheek.

"Hi, I brought you some chocolates." Lilian blushed and stepped inside.

She followed William. The hallway had living rooms either side decorated in shades of white and fawn.

William slotted himself back behind the island counter and put her gift in the fridge. He gestured to Lilian to take a seat on the bar stool opposite.

"I'm just finishing the pizza dough then I'll give you a tour. How was your debate?" William asked, splitting his attention between Lilian and their lunch.

"Good. The Deakin team were better than we were expecting, but we still won." Lilian smiled proudly. Her new skills had pushed them over the line.

William poured yeast into flour and folded the mixture with a fork.

"Congratulations. Would you like something to drink? Tea, coffee, beer, wine, milk, juice, water?"

"Juice would be great, thanks. I don't drink alcohol."

William consulted the fridge door. "We've got orange or blackcurrant?"

"Orange, please," Lilian replied, glad he didn't seem fazed she was a teetotaller.

William heaped the dough onto a marble benchtop and started kneading.

"Your house is beautiful," Lilian commented, admiring the sophisticated pallet.

"Thanks. We've lived here my whole life. Every year my mother changes the décor then it feels like a different house. Keeps things interesting."

"Do you have siblings?" Lilian couldn't remember Doug ever mentioning any other nieces or nephews.

"No, my parents met in their late thirties. I'm lucky to be here!" William joked. "What about you? I think I saw your brother at Lily's party?"

"There's two of them," Lilian clarified. "Marcus and Tim are identical twins, they're the youngest. Ari's in the middle."

"So, you're the oldest," William commented while he cut dough into portions and rolled it into balls.

"I am. My father died when we were young, so I took care of them a lot when they were little."

"I remember. Lily went up to Sydney to look after you guys for ages. The Marina was pretty quiet without her."

Lilian felt awkward that he already knew so much about her family.

William covered the tray with a damp tea towel and set an egg timer.

"Do you feel like you already know me?"

William put the empty mixing bowl in the sink, removed his apron, then reached for her hand.

"Anything I know about you is from Lily. I still want to hear your perspective," William assured her tenderly. "Ready for the tour?"

Lilian nodded.

William kept her hand in his and led Lilian up the stairs. "The bedrooms and the study are on the first floor."

Lilian glimpsed immaculately made beds overflowing with dress pillows.

William stopped at the last room at the end of the landing. "This is my room."

Designated dark and pale blues, it looked like a guest bedroom. Lilian wasn't surprised, William hadn't lived there for years.

He led Lilian back down the stairs and showed her the backyard, the boatshed, and the living rooms, then circled back to the kitchen.

"I didn't realise you were into surfing." Lilian had noticed a surfboard collection stacked up against the side of the house.

"I was raised on the water, swimming, sailing, surfing. Most things we do as a family are in, or on, the water. Mum and Dad are away fishing this weekend. What about you?"

William poured himself a blackcurrant juice and sat on a bar stool next to Lilian.

"I'm not very sporty. I walk mostly, along the beach." Lilian felt self-conscious. William seemed to have an idyllic life. She felt inadequate.

"I love walking. Why don't we go for a walk after we eat?"

"That would be great." Lilian blushed, flattered William wanted to spend the whole day with her. She pointed at the pizza dough. "This is impressive."

"I do most of the cooking, my parents work long hours. I cooked them dinner most nights during high school."

"Was it lonely? Do you wish you'd had a brother or sister around?" Lilian hoped her presumption wasn't saddening.

William considered her question thoughtfully. "I was never lonely. I was always surrounded by family and friends. But I wouldn't want to have an only child. My parents wanted to have more, it's not something I ever resented."

"You want kids?"

"If it happens, it happens. Mum wants to be a grandmother, but she hasn't started to pressure me… yet," William joked. "Do you want to be a mother?"

Lilian was distracted by the heat from his palm resting on her knee.

"I can't imagine not having children, but I've never thought about being a parent," Lilian admitted, locked on his eyes.

William was magnetic when he was focusing on her.

The kitchen timer buzzed. Startled, Lilian nearly spilt her orange juice.

William detached from her and re-aproned while examining the dough. "I have no doubt you'll be a wonderful mother."

24

"Sorry, it's convoluted," Lilian explained, as Jamie drove them to Wilderness Warriors.

"No, it makes complete sense. We're going to spend the day picking up rubbish, with a guy who hates you, because of an agreement you made to avoid listening to your friend complain about a relationship that she's no longer in," Jamie teased.

"You make the situation sound far more absurd than it is." Lilian laughed, embarrassed by her preposterous deal with Jane.

"I think I make it sound the right amount of ridiculous," Jamie mocked playfully. "Is Jane the drunk one who abandoned you in Newcastle?"

Jamie pulled over to the shoulder to check they were on the right road.

"Yes, that's Jane. You've probably seen us together around campus."

"I don't take much notice of anyone else when you're around," Jamie flirted.

Lilian blushed.

Not wanting to distract Jamie while he was navigating, she looked out the window and admired the gumtrees until they were back on the road.

"It's weird our friendship came about because we happened

to be in that pub on the same night." Lilian chose her phrasing carefully.

Jamie supressed a grin. "I'd been planning on asking you out for a while. Although, you might not have said yes if we hadn't spent so much time together."

"Really, you've known me for years. Why now?" Lilian was amazed he'd thought of her at all before Newcastle.

"I had a girlfriend. Then I was single for a while and not really interested in dating. Let's just say, I've always been aware of you." Jamie smiled, trying to be honest but not creepy.

"I didn't realise you had a girlfriend. Why did you two break up?"

"We'd been together since high school and I knew I didn't want to marry her. It was unfair to stay in the relationship, I was preventing her from meeting someone else."

"That's considerate." Lilian assumed there was more to the story but was content with the summary.

"She's a great person. She's already engaged. That's what she wanted, it just wasn't me."

Given Jamie's clear residual fondness for his ex, Lilian was glad to know she wouldn't have to worry about a resurgence.

"What about you?"

"I haven't been in a relationship."

If Jamie was deterred by her inexperience, there was nothing she could do to change the truth. Nevertheless, Lilian didn't want to elaborate.

"Do you think you'll travel after you graduate?" she said.

Jamie smiled, enamoured by Lilian's bashfulness. "I'm starting fulltime at the firm the day after my last exam. I might take a few weeks off and head north next winter."

"You don't want a holiday before starting work... forever?" Lilian was surprised. She needed a break.

"No way. I'd be bored out of my mind. I'm up at five, I'm not sure what I'd do for," Jamie paused to calculate, "sixteen hours a day, if I wasn't working."

Lilian felt daunted by his boundless energy.

"How did your ex like getting up that early?" she blurted before she could stop herself.

"She got up and ran with me." Jamie laughed. "If you're going to break up with me because I get up too early, I'd be willing to consider a negotiation."

Lilian was momentarily unnerved by Jamie's inference they were in a relationship, then decided to leave the comment. They hadn't even kissed yet.

Mindful she'd dragged them back into ex-territory, Lilian changed the subject, again. "I'm thinking about travelling. My sister's in Europe, and she's been trying to convince me to join her. Most of the graduate programs I've applied for start next year, so I have time."

"What's stopping you?" Jamie asked, noticing Lilian's hesitation.

"I'm just not sure whether I should spend all my savings on someone else's adventure. I'm waiting until after my interviews to decide. Once I know whether I have a job, and when it starts, I think I'll feel more certain."

"Good plan," Jamie remarked.

Vikram was standing at the entrance to the national park, handing out equipment, with what appeared to be a new girlfriend draped around his shoulders.

Lilian pointed. "That's Vikram."

Jamie parked and they began changing into their gumboots.

"Thanks again for helping today. Vikram is far less likely to chastise Jane about the fate of humanity if the volume of rubbish collected is not impacted by her absence."

"No problem, any excuse to spend time with you." Jamie squeezed Lilian's hand. "Before I forget, my firm is hosting drinks after work next week. I'd love it if you would come?"

Lilian glowed. Jamie's grin was contagious. "I'll check my calendar, but I'm sure I can make it."

25

The sun was hovering over the horizon as Lilian and William walked along the beach toward Fitzroy Street.

"How's your house hunting going?" Lilian asked.

William had been scouring Bendigo rental listings at work.

"Well. I'm heading up next week to look at a couple of units near the hospital. You're welcome to join me?" William suggested casually.

"That sounds fun, but I have to study for exams," Lilian apologised.

"No worries. Maybe you'll have time to visit after you've graduated?" William replied, hopefully.

"I might be heading overseas to meet up with Ari," Lilian said, sidestepping he open-ended invitation, uncertain about their future.

"That's exciting. I backpacked around Asia for six months in the middle of my degree. It was amazing, I'm so glad I went."

Lilian wasn't sure whether he was encouraging her to take the trip.

"It wouldn't bother you if I left?" Lilian queried, trying not to sound needy.

"This feels like a trick question." William laughed and took her hand. "What's the right answer?"

"No tricks. I'm just curious." Lilian smiled.

He gave her a suspicious glance. "I would never try and dissuade you from travelling if that's what you want to do."

Lilian watched the final sliver of sun sink below the skyline.

William felt like Lilian was holding back. She was clearly stewing over something. "We've got some time before the movie. Shall we sit for a few minutes?"

"Sure," Lilian agreed, and they walked over to a bench adjacent to the sand and faced the city.

Lilian shivered.

"Are you cold?"

The night air was cooler down by the water than up on the Esplanade. Lilian hadn't brought a jacket. "A bit."

"I'm warm, I can hug you if you want?" William offered and put his arm around her.

He could see Lilian was thinking about something and waited for her to speak.

"Did you have a girlfriend when you were in Perth?" Lilian said, finally revealing her worries.

William didn't mind the question, he had nothing to hide. "I broke up with someone before I left. It wasn't serious."

"Because of the distance?" Lilian asked, trying to ascertain whether William's ex was still in his life, and his heart.

She sat up and turned to face him.

"No. We had been together for a few years, she wanted to move to Melbourne with me, but I didn't want to make a commitment," William explained simply. There was nothing to elaborate.

"Yet here I am," Lilian said, unsure what to make of his explanation.

"Yes, you are." William smiled affectionately and ran his warm hands over her chilly arms. "Not what I expected."

"So, this is different somehow?" Lilian flicked a pointed finger between them.

"I knew I was moving to Bendigo. I knew you were studying. I thought it probably wasn't good timing, but you asked me out and I'm happy you did."

"I'm not sure what to make of that," Lilian said, starting to feel upset.

"Sorry, let me try again. You're the first person I've met that I feel like I could fall in love with. But we don't know each other very well yet and I'm not in a hurry. I wasn't expecting this, but I wouldn't be anywhere else."

William hoped he'd imparted how rare it was for him to feel this way.

"This is too much for me to deal with at the moment. I don't know where I'll be in a few months, and you're leaving." Lilian stopped speaking abruptly, captured by her next thought.

William cupped her cheek softly, nervous that Lilian was going to end things. "While we're both still in Melbourne I'd like to see you as much as I can. That's all. Is that okay for you?"

She considered his proposition. "I would like that, but I've got interviews this week, then exams, and work at the Marina."

"I know you have other priorities. I'm here if you need me," William assured her supportively. He knew she had no spare time. He was hoping for an upgrade.

"Thanks." Lilian felt drained. "I'm exhausted and cold. Do you mind if we skip the movie? We could go back to the terrace and hang out in the library?"

"I would love that, even better." William smiled, relieved to have survived the conversation.

He wrapped himself around Lilian, and they walked back to the terrace in each other's arms.

26

"Mum, sorry I'm late! My lecture ran over," Lilian huffed, flustered. She'd missed the tram and run all the way from Bourke Street.

Dorothy had already ordered a latte from the café under the train station.

A waiter came over with Dorothy's drink and Lilian ordered peppermint tea.

"No problem. I have an hour. I checked out early," Dorothy said dryly. Lilian didn't notice the bite.

Dorothy had opted to stay in a serviced apartment over Southbank so as not to disrupt Lilian's routine leading up to exams. Lilian had insisted on meeting Dorothy before her mother flew back to Sydney.

"Are you excited to be going home? Tim isn't coping without you at all," Lilian asked.

After Lily's birthday party, Dorothy had been consumed by an inexplicable need to be close to her mother. So, she stayed. It was the longest time Dorothy could remember being in Melbourne since leaving with Eric after their wedding. It was also the longest time she'd been away from the twins. Freedom was as confronting as it was liberating.

"I miss the boys, but it doesn't feel like I'm going home. It feels like I'm leaving home."

"Lily would love you to move back," Lilian said excitedly.

"And what about you?" Dorothy snapped.

Lilian had seemed entirely unfazed by Dorothy's extended presence in Melbourne, and they'd not spent any time together without Lily.

Lilian was startled by her tone.

"I love you being in Melbourne, but I don't know where I'll end up after I graduate," Lilian said, not used to being challenged by her mother.

Dorothy regained her composure and changed the subject. "Have you picked a boyfriend yet?"

Lilian smiled shyly. "They're both amazing, I can't decide who I like more."

"I met William briefly at the Marina, he's quite handsome. I assume Jamie is as attractive?" Dorothy was privately irritated that Lilian's already heavy schedule was further constrained by dating.

Lilian frowned disapprovingly at Dorothy's reduction.

Dorothy was used to having these conversations with Ari. It was her first time discussing a boyfriend with Lilian. She wasn't sure how to talk to her serious daughter about love or sex.

"They're the same age, they both want to get married and have kids. They both have an ex that they broke up with. They're both starting great graduate positions. But the way I feel when I'm with them is completely different. I just can't figure out why," Lilian explained, throwing her hands up in the air, nearly knocking a water glass off the table.

"Who's the better kisser?" Dorothy asked.

Lilian blushed.

"I don't know, I haven't kissed either of them. I've spent more time with Jamie because of debating but we're always around other people. Same with William. When I see him, we're usually at work," Lilian said defensively, presuming her mother was judging her patience.

"Well, there are worse problems to have." Dorothy laughed cautiously.

Lilian was bothered that their conversation had become so strained. Dorothy seemed annoyed.

"Mum, are you alright?" Lilian asked. She didn't want Dorothy to leave Melbourne perturbed.

"I'm fine." Dorothy felt guilty for taking her emotions out on Lilian. "This is the first time I've been alone since you were born. I don't think I've been apart from one of the four of you for even one night. I just wish I'd seen more of you while I was here, that's all."

Dorothy looked hurt, an expression new to Lilian.

"I'm sorry. I can come up to Sydney once I've graduated. I didn't realise… I didn't realise you were lonely."

The comment was cutting. Even after weeks alone, Dorothy hadn't grasped that she was experiencing loneliness. Lilian was right. She had been feeling acutely the distance between her mother and her children.

"That's not your responsibility. Promise me you won't worry about me after I leave. You need to focus on enjoying this time before you graduate." Dorothy welled with shame for burdening her already overstretched daughter.

"I promise not to worry about you, if you promise to see your doctor," Lilian negotiated sternly.

Dorothy laughed. Only her sensible eldest would prescribe a doctor for loneliness. Ari would have told Dorothy to find a husband.

"I promise, and I would love for you to visit after you graduate. I can't remember the last time we had more than a week together since you left. And you can bring your boyfriend too, once you've picked one," Dorothy joked.

Lilian sighed, relieved they were back in sync.

"Ugh, it's going to be awful. I have no idea how to make this decision." Lilian hesitated, not wanting to exacerbate Dorothy's sorrow. "How did you know Dad was the one?"

"Eric was never a choice. I was his from the moment we met. I wish I'd spent more time over the years remembering the good times." Dorothy smiled at the memory of desperate passion during their first months together. "When you know, you'll know."

27

The foyer was overflowing with important seeming people deep in conversation, huddled over laptops and notepads. Feeling misplaced in a cocktail dress, Lilian entered the concourse, walking against a sea of suits.

Jamie was holding the elevator. She'd never seen him in corporate attire and was impressed by his style.

"Hi, beautiful." Jamie kissed her cheek.

Lilian could smell cologne. Between his outfit and lawyerly confidence, she felt like she was meeting him for the first time.

"You look amazing," he said.

"Thanks, you also look, very, amazing," Lilian spluttered.

"Really?" Jamie teased, leading her into one of the elevators.

"You just look so different?" Lilian laughed, mortified by her nervous incoherence.

"I tone it down at uni," Jamie replied graciously. "How was the interview?"

"It was great, I'm so relieved it's over." The lift pinged and the doors flew open. The noise from the party drowned the end of her sentence.

Jamie's colleagues were gathered on the other side of an island reception, champagne and canapes in hand. Only a few dozen people had arrived, but the space amplified the chatter, and it echoed like they were in a stadium.

Lilian's eyes adjusted to the dim lighting and she tried to calm her nerves.

"I will probably be pulled away from you all night, but don't worry. Everyone is super friendly and they're really excited to meet you," Jamie advised belatedly.

"No problem," Lilian said, feigning preparedness.

With his arm around Lilian's waist, Jamie led her to the bar and she ordered a soda with lime.

He was distracted, scanning the room.

"Who are you looking for?"

"My boss. She's heading home soon but she wanted to meet you."

Before Lilian could reply, Jamie had begun manoeuvring her toward a high table next to the window.

Two impeccably presented women were sipping white wine. Jamie put his hand on one of their backs and instantly transformed into the performer Lilian knew from debating.

"Sorry to interrupt, Carmen. I wanted to make sure you had a chance to meet Lilian before you left."

"Jamie, of course. Hello, you must be Lilian." Carmen smiled and shook Lilian's hand.

Lilian found immaculate dressers intimidating. Carmen however seemed genuinely welcoming.

"Would you like to sit with us while Jamie entertains one of his new clients?" Carmen offered.

Lilian gratefully accepted the seat.

"I won't be too long," Jamie assured her and disappeared into the thick of lawyers.

Lilian was awed by the breathtaking view of the city from the top floor.

"It's great to finally meet you. Jamie mentioned you had an interview today?" Carmen recalled.

Lilian was momentarily taken aback by Carmen's knowledge of her day. "I did, with Bendigo Bank. I'm graduating at the end of the year. I've been interviewing for graduate positions."

"I understand from Jamie you're specialising in tax law?" Carmen consulted her colleague, who nodded.

Apparently Jamie was talking about Lilian to the whole office.

"Yes, I have my meeting with the Australian Tax Office next week," Lilian confirmed, surrendering to the celebrity of dating Jamie.

"Congratulations. Getting an interview is half the battle." Carmen winked supportively.

Having been unable to find his client, Jamie returned. The other lawyer offered Jamie her seat and went in search of champagne.

"Jamie, your girlfriend is lovely. How did you two meet?" Carmen asked, approval granted.

Lilian was alarmed by the misrepresentation but kept smiling, unsure whether Jamie had registered Carmen's mistake.

"Lilian and I are in the debating club together. She's a spectacular First Chair," Jamie boasted and placed his arm around Lilian.

"He's being modest. Jamie taught me everything I know," Lilian added playfully, careful not to embarrass him in front of Carmen.

"I have no doubt. Jamie is our most outstanding junior

lawyer. We can't wait to have him here fulltime." Carmen patted Jamie on the shoulder. "Jamie, the kids are waiting for me. Lilian, I hope we'll see you around here more often."

"Thanks, Carmen," Lilian reciprocated dutifully.

Once Carmen had left, Jamie returned to his usual self.

"Sorry, I never told them you were my girlfriend. I just talk about you all the time. They must have assumed." He grinned gingerly.

"I don't mind people knowing we're dating," Lilian replied diplomatically, wishing Jamie wouldn't press her on the title.

"I was hoping you would say you don't mind being my girlfriend," Jamie replied cheekily, leaning in for a kiss.

It was a cute moment, but Lilian wasn't going to default into a relationship on account of incorrect office gossip.

"We're just dating, Jamie," she said sternly, rejecting his affection.

Oblivious to the crowd staring at them, Jamie respectfully removed his arm, undeterred by the setback. "You're worth the wait."

28

Lilian opened the front door to find an enormous bunch of red and pink roses laying on the step. The card was printed with her name.

Irritated, she grabbed the flowers and reversed. She was completely focused on her interview and had no interest in being romanced this morning.

Lilian threw the bouquet at the couch then pivoted at lightspeed, hoping to still make her tram.

With one hand on the front door handle, she was paralysed by a blood curdling scream followed by a thud.

Lilian's heart stopped and she sprinted back up the hallway, through Lily's bedroom, and into the ensuite.

Lily was twisted on the tiles in her silk robe, holding her leg.

"I'm okay, it's just my ankle," Lily whimpered through streaming tears.

"You are not okay! Don't move, I'll get the ice." Lilian ran back to where she'd dropped her bag and grabbed her phone.

On the way to the kitchen to get the peas from the freezer, she called William. He answered and began to speak but she cut him off.

"Lily had a fall. Can you come over?" Lilian huffed urgently.

She had been mentally preparing for this day since she had

arrived in Melbourne, although she had thought it would be a hip.

"Call an ambulance!" William cried, alarmed.

"She says it's just her ankle, but I'm worried it's worse. She looks like she's in a lot of pain," Lilian pleaded, wrapping the peas in a tea towel.

"I'm at the Marina, I'll be there in five. Ice and elevate if you can. Don't move her if she's in pain. Don't give her any medication," William instructed and hung up.

Lilian tucked her phone in the band of her suit skirt and went to wedge the front door open. Then she took the quilt off the bed and gently wrapped it around Lily.

"William's coming over to check your ankle, he said for us to wait here," Lilian relayed as she sat down next to the shower and placed the peas on Lily's ankle.

Lily yelped. "You need to leave. You're going to miss your interview. I'll be fine."

"Absolutely not! If the Tax Office have a problem rescheduling because I need to take care of you then I don't want to work for them!" Lilian argued, taking off her suit jacket and hanging it over the towel rack. "William said to elevate. Do you think you can lift your foot off the ground?"

Lily was sitting with her back against the sink cabinet with her injured leg stretched out.

Lilian's heart broke at the frailty of her normally vivacious grandmother.

"I don't think so," Lily said, fighting to hold back sobs. "What are you doing here? I thought I heard you leave?"

Lilian had completely forgotten about the gift.

"I did. Someone sent roses, so I came back in." Lilian rotated the peas.

"That's sweet. Which boyfriend?" Lily teased, grateful for the distraction.

"I don't know, I didn't read the card."

"Where did you put the flowers? You'd better hide them before William gets here. They might be from Jamie." Lily laughed through gritted teeth.

"I'm not leaving you," Lilian retorted, apparently the only one of them with proportionate priorities.

Before Lily could respond, William materialised in the bedroom.

"I could hear you laughing from the hallway." He smiled, relieved his patient was in good spirits. "Do you mind if I take a look?"

"Hi, let me get out the way." Lilian collected her jacket and phone and vacated the small bathroom.

"Darling, thank you for coming to rescue me," Lily said to William as he crouched down beside her and started his examination.

"No problem, Lily," William replied, concentrating. "Can you feel me squeezing your toes?"

"Yes," Lily replied obediently.

"Is this painful?" he added.

"Yes." Lily winced.

"What about the rest of your leg? Where did you land when you fell?" William checked Lily's reflexes.

"After I twisted my ankle, I caught the towel rail before I hit the ground. It could have been a lot worse."

William inspected the swelling. "Do you think you can stand?"

"No, I don't think the pain would allow it," Lily's said, finally acknowledging she had been badly hurt.

"That's alright, you don't need to move. It looks like a sprain, but it may be broken. You need an X-ray. Are you happy for me to call an ambulance for you?"

"Only if you promise to wait with me. Lilian needs to go to her interview. Now!" Lily stated, firmly.

"Lily, it would be my pleasure," William said warmly and turned to face Lilian, doubting she would leave.

"I'm not going," Lilian cried, exasperated.

"Well I'm not going to the hospital, unless you go to your interview," Lily retorted fiercely.

Lilian knew that tone, her grandmother was famously stubborn.

"I can stay. Brett can open without me. Go, please, really, we're fine here." William nodded encouragingly.

"In fact, I would prefer William. He's a doctor."

Lilian stood unflinching in the ensuite doorway.

"Lilian, you are upsetting me," Lily shouted, becoming distressed.

"Okay, I'll go," Lilian surrendered, redonning her suit jacket.

William settled on the bathroom floor and took out his phone to call for a transfer.

"Lilian, can you please fetch William and I some water before you leave," Lily requested victoriously.

"Of course," Lilian replied and dashed to the kitchen.

She placed the jug under the tap and collected two glasses. As the water ran, she picked the bouquet off the floor and read the message. The flowers were from Jamie. She stuffed them into the back of the corner cabinet, behind the cereal boxes, and returned to the bathroom.

William was on the phone explaining Lily's condition to the operator while taking her pulse.

Lilian placed the jug on the floor within Lily's reach.

"We're all sorted. I'll text you with updates," William said, trying to reassure Lilian who was struggling to leave.

"Go!" Lily yelled.

"Okay, I'm going. Do you need anything else?" Lilian stalled.

"No, darling. Good luck." Lily dismissed Lilian with a wink.

"From Jamie," Lilian whispered, then kissed Lily's forehead, grabbed her bag and raced, again, out the front door.

29

Lilian sat in the waiting room outside Professor Matthews' office. The walls were lined with certificates.

Lilian had been horrified when she'd received the call advising there were several issues the professor wanted to discuss. Lilian had never been summoned to a disciplinary meeting and had agonised over possible reasons. She hadn't missed any classes or assignments and Jane hadn't made a scene recently.

An assistant signalled for Lilian to enter.

"Morning, Lilian. Please take a seat. Wherever you like," Professor Matthews said from behind a grand redwood desk surrounded by bookcases crammed with texts from floor to ceiling.

There was a couch, a small round table with chairs, and a leather armchair opposite the desk. Overwhelmed, Lilian froze, staring at the multitude of seating options.

"Opposite the desk is fine." The professor was used to visitors being intimidated by her status.

"You have a lot of awards," Lilian commented redundantly.

"Yes, I have," Professor Matthews agreed. "Lilian, thanks for agreeing to a meeting. We have a few different matters to address."

"Good or bad?" Lilian asked, impatient and nervous.

"Informative and pre-emptive."

"I don't know what that means."

"We will get to everything," Professor Matthews assured her, appreciating how stressful these confrontations were for her students. "I have been contacted by both the Australian Tax Office and Bendigo Bank to verify the written references I provided for your graduate applications. Both were impressed by your interview."

"Wow, that's great news, I haven't heard from either of them." Lilian's apprehension dissipated.

The professor's smile quickly hardened. "I am however concerned about your progress this semester."

"Really?" Lilian's relief vanished.

"Your marks are lower than I expected and your concentration has been… patchy."

"I didn't realise," Lilian said, abashed.

The assistant buzzed in with a phone call and Professor Matthews instructed them to take a message.

"Lilian, I have been doing this a long time. I assume there's a boy involved," the professor stated the question.

"I have been dating, but not at the expense of my studies," Lilian defended, mortified.

"Lilian, you're not failing but based on your declining attention, I doubt you will be able to perform to your usual exceptional standard in the exam." The professor pointed to a trophy on her desk.

"I…" Lilian began to respond.

"Lilian, I didn't invite you here for an explanation. I merely hope you correct your course."

Lilian conceded the warning. "Thank you, Professor."

"You're most welcome. It would seem you are going to have to make some defining decisions shortly. Have you thought about which job offer you would accept?" Professor Matthews' expression softened.

"I haven't decided," Lilian replied, embarrassed that she had been preoccupied with her romantic dilemma.

"It will be a shame for us to lose you to another city." Professor Matthews' brightest graduates were often sought by the Tax Headquarters in Canberra.

"I have applied to a few other banks and firms here and in Sydney."

"I see, and do you have a preference?" The professor began preparing for her next appointment.

"The Tax Office is my first choice, but my family are in Sydney. It would be nice to be able to see them more often," Lilian explained, feeling obliged to justify considering abandoning Melbourne.

"Very well. The Tax Office would be an outstanding start to your career. I hope the Commissioner has the sense to snap you up early," Professor Matthews said encouragingly and nodded to the door.

"Thank you, Professor. I'm sorry to have disappointed you. I will work harder," Lilian apologised sheepishly as she stood up, shaken from the admonishing.

"Lilian, it's not a disappointment to me that you have befallen adoration. But any man worth your time would not begrudge you needing to focus on your studies." The professor chuckled. "Legal wisdom is but one form of knowledge. I think it was Paul Kelly who sang that love never runs on time."

30

The bruise from Lily's sprain had caused her calf to turn a vibrant shade of purple. As a result, she had been showered with get-well presents and the terrace now resembled a florist.

Her doctor had instructed Lily to stay in bed until she was completely healed, which was expected to take at least a month. Ruth, Brett and Jane had been coming over to help care for her.

"Stop, both of you! I've had enough of your incessant speculating," Lilian chided. With no space to herself, she was feeling agitated.

Jane had just finished her watch and was lying on Lily's bed as they ate dinner together from trays.

"I reject your trivialisation, Lilian. This is an extremely important decision. One which deserves thorough consideration," Lily refuted, trying to sound lawyerly.

They had picked sides. Lily had been advocating for William and Jane was team Jamie.

"I'm not denying the importance of the decision, I'm telling you both to butt out. Professor Matthews told me I needed to focus on studying and you two are not helping. Mum said when I know, I'll know. So that's my approach from now on."

"How will you know that you know when you know?" Jane questioned cheekily, dissolving into laughter.

Lilian sat on the floor, defeated in her attempts to change the topic. "Isn't it time for you to go home?"

"Sorry, darling. We were just having some fun. We'll stop, won't we, Jane," Lily promised, sharing a smirk with Jane.

"I will stop, after one last question. Do you think either of them is dating anyone else?" Jane posed genuinely.

Lilian collected their empty plates.

"We haven't discussed it, but I doubt they are," she stated with conviction, appreciating the irony.

"Would you mind?" Jane persisted.

Lilian hadn't thought about it. "I don't think it's any of my business."

"You wouldn't be jealous?" Lily interjected, intrigued by Jane's line of inquiry.

"I would be understanding of the inherent principle of dating, one is not yet prepared to make a commitment," Lilian replied defensively.

"That's lawyer speak for I'd be jealous," Jane interpreted for Lily who was enthralled by her granddaughter's determination to rationalise passion.

Lilian snapped, fed up with both of them. "I don't know if I'd be jealous. I don't know whether they will move on before I'm ready. I don't know who I like more. I don't know where I will get a job. Is there anything else that I don't know that we should hypothesise about tonight?"

Jane took the plates from Lilian.

"I'm not used to being the composed one in this friendship," Jane joked to Lily. "Walk me to the tram?"

Lilian turned to Lily to check she would be alright alone.

"I'm fine, darling. Thanks for coming today, Jane." Lily was getting better at accepting assistance.

"Anytime, Lily. I'll see you in a few days."

They left the dishes in the kitchen. Jane collected her backpack, and they hit the footpath.

The salty air was refreshing.

"What a fun night. Sorry we were teasing you. I know how much you hate girl talk." Jane giggled. She had started to look happy again.

"I don't hate girl talk, I just find it extremely unhelpful and a complete waste of time," Lilian replied. "Enough about me, have you heard from Luke?"

Jane hadn't mentioned Luke since their dinner party after the breakup.

"I have," Jane confirmed furtively.

"And?"

"His new girlfriend broke up with him after about a week, as you predicted," Jane imparted flatly.

"Wow, and you didn't think to mention that during, oh, any of the times I've seen you since then?"

"I didn't think you would want to know. You didn't want to hear about Luke when we were together. Why would you want to hear about him now?" Jane alleged with a tinge of hurt.

"Fair point. I'm sorry. I feel like I've been derelict in my friendship duties. I want to be there to support you if you're upset. From now on, can you please just tell me if something like that happens?" Lilian requested, ashamed of her former intolerance for Jane's messy problems.

"There's nothing to tell. I blocked his number. I'm properly done with him. But still, thanks. I would like that," Jane said bittersweetly.

"What changed?"

"To be honest, I think talking about Jamie and William all semester has made me crave something more mature. Not mature boring, just, mature stable." Jane laughed. "After all these years, you finally made me sensible."

"I can't believe you just said you want a mature relationship," Lilian marvelled, impressed by Jane's newfound resolve. If she had been sitting, Lilian might have fallen off her chair.

31

Lilian locked the Marina's front door behind the last of the diners and went to find William.

She knocked at his open office door. "Can I come in for a work chat?"

William looked tired.

"Sure, what's a work chat?" he joked.

Lilian ignored his levity and sat down at the opposite side of the desk. It felt too far away.

"I was hoping to take a few weeks off. I got in trouble from one of my professors. I have exams coming up and I need to study."

"Take a few weeks off from work or from me?"

She had meant work but the prospect of having one less commitment was instantly lightening. Lilian recalled Professor Matthews' advice that good men wait.

"Both, if that's alright? Also, I will need to resign if I get a full-time job, or if I end up travelling, so I don't know when I'll be available for shifts again," Lilian added, embarrassed by how demanding she sounded. She felt awful abandoning her colleagues while Doug was away.

"First, if you need a few weeks off that's fine. Second, if you need to resign, then just give me as much notice as you can."

William walked around the desk and sat next to her. "Third, I understand you need to focus on studying, but I'd love one last date before you go dark."

"Thank you." Lilian frowned disbelievingly, he was being so accommodating while she was being so vague.

"Is that yes to the date?" William laughed.

"Yes, I would love that," Lilian agreed happily amidst a rush of relief.

"So potentially, this might be your last shift," William remarked.

Lilian hadn't realised but he was right. If she got a job which started immediately, she wouldn't work at the Marina again.

Sadness enveloped her. "I'm not ready."

When she had moved to Melbourne, Brett had practically adopted her, and Coen was like a big brother. Lilian couldn't fathom her life without them weaving in and out of her weeks.

"Don't worry. Brett won't let you leave without a party. The regulars are going to be devastated. I'll have to start dropping hints slowly. I don't want any pensioner heart attacks," William teased, only half joking.

"I've had enough pensioner medical drama to last me a lifetime," Lilian agreed.

William's stare was intense, it made Lilian self-conscious. "What?"

"Nothing, I just can't picture you getting told off? You're the hardest worker here."

"It happened. One of the pre-eminent legal thinkers of her generation told me to stop daydreaming about boys," Lilian paraphrased, remembering how mortified she'd been.

"What were you daydreaming about?" William grinned.

"I wasn't daydreaming about anything. She'd just sensed I was distracted and assumed it was because of a boy." Lilian managed to keep a straight face.

"You don't have to dream about me all day. I'm right here." William pointed to himself, smugly, and tried to give Lilian a hug.

Lilian didn't want Brett to catch them in a compromising embrace. Brett hadn't warmed to William yet, and Lilian had been avoiding telling him they were dating. She knew Brett was going to react badly.

"You stay in your chair." Lilian playfully jumped away from his outstretch arms. "I'm going home. I look forward to our date."

"Give Lily my love." William laughed and went back to the boss side of the desk.

"I will not. She's had enough excitement for one week. Thanks for the study leave." Lilian blew William a kiss then circled back to the staffroom to wait for Brett.

Everyone else had gone home for the night and the staffroom was empty. Lilian pre-emptively cleared out her locker. Once she was done, Lilian sat alone in the quiet and allowed her worries to surface.

She hadn't planned a break from Jamie or William, but it felt right to put that contest on hold to focus on exams, and her future.

Brett burst into the staffroom, disrupting her thoughts.

"Ready to go?" he asked, hauling cooler bags full of lunches for Lily.

Lilian sighed heavily. "Not really, but I'm prepared."

32

"I still don't understand why you think it's rewarding?" Lilian remained bemused by Jamie's adoration of contract law.

"If you can't understand the sweet satisfaction of a perfectly crafted contract, I can't help you," Jamie said, sprawled across the picnic blanket.

"Then I am beyond saving," Lilian flirted, plucking an olive from the antipasto platter Jamie had brought.

"I feel the same way about tax law. We will have to agree to disagree." Jamie reached around the sparkling apple juice to hold her hand. "I'm going to miss you."

"You also have exams," Lilian noted.

"I know, it just felt like we were getting closer?" Jamie suggested hopefully.

"Jamie, I need to focus on studying." Lilian appreciated his frustration. "This is a lovely last date, for now."

The botanic gardens were dusted with brightly coloured petals. The pond was shimmering, ducks floated between the reeds. The setting was quintessential, Lilian felt like she was posing in a painting.

"I've been meaning to ask you something, but you're probably going to think it's a weird question."

"Try me," Jamie challenged.

"The first time I saw you competing, you won a debate about a sandwich."

"That was years ago," Jamie recollected, intrigued. "Whether or not sandwiches should have crusts, if I recall correctly."

"You argued that sandwiches shouldn't have crusts. I was wondering if you actually believe that?"

Jamie laughed. "I like crusts."

Lilian smiled, contented.

"What are you really asking me?" he inquired, suspiciously.

"It's not a loaded question. I just remember at the time being amazed by your conviction. I thought maybe it was because you really preferred your sandwiches without crusts," Lilian admitted bashfully.

"So, you're worried you won't be able to tell when I'm lying?" Jamie considered Lilian doubtfully.

"No, I'm not worried about that. I know I won't be able to tell when you're lying." Lilian laughed.

"It's a strange thing to have remembered," Jamie smiled half-heartedly.

"Honestly, I was just curious."

Certain he was missing the insinuation. Jamie appeared to tense.

"Okay, how do I fix this? You look like I just shattered your dreams."

He let go of her hand.

"I'm fine, I just wish you'd be more vulnerable with me. I would hope there were things you worried about," Jamie admitted.

"So, you think because I'm not worried, I don't care?" Lilian asked, baffled by his complexity.

"In a relationship you need to be able to trust that the other person is going to come to you with their fears so you can work it out together. You can trust that I will tell you the things that scare me."

She decided not to point out they weren't in a relationship. "You really are good at this."

Jamie looked impatient for her to be serious.

"I'm not worried about anything because I've been too busy to think about what a future with you would look like," Lilian said, trying not to worsen the situation.

"Thank you." Jamie smiled, appreciating her invested response. "Anything else?"

Lilian did have niggling apprehensions but didn't want to spoil the picnic.

"I do find your lifestyle to be quite intense." Lilian felt absurd being needlessly critical of Jamie to prove her affection.

"I knew you didn't want to get up at five," he teased, glad she was finally opening up.

"No, I don't mean that. You have so many people in your life, and they all seem to have demands on you, and dreams for your future. I guess I'm not sure where I would fit in? It feels like… you're full."

"Ouch. Perhaps it feels like that because everything we've done has been me inviting you into my life. I'd love to meet Lily and Jane and visit you at the Marina."

Lilian hadn't been purposely keeping Jamie away, but she felt like he was trying to discredit the legitimacy of her concerns.

"This is a great example of why I need space for a few weeks.

This doesn't matter to me right now, having a hypothetical relationship discussion is the furthest thing from my mind," Lilian joked light-heartedly, trying to mask her irritation.

"You're right, I'm sorry," Jamie said, realising too late it was the wrong time to push her.

"No, don't be sorry. I've never been in a relationship before. I don't need to work through my problems with someone else. I solve my problems myself, and I don't feel the need to share every thought that runs through my head."

"I understand," Jamie said, backpedaling.

"But I don't think you do," Lilian said frankly. "Being someone's wife is not on my bucket list. I feel stressed by the pressure of having to live up to the expectations everyone else will have of me if I was with you."

Jamie moved the picnic basket from between them and shuffled over to put his arm around her. "Seems like you were worrying about something."

"No, I wasn't thinking about it at all," Lilian said, annoyed by his persistent belief she was hiding something.

"I have always had this kind of attention because of my parents but I appreciate it would be daunting if you're not used to it," Jamie empathised.

"I get that but I really hadn't thought about it," Lilian insisted strenuously.

"Look, I can't pretend my life doesn't come without interest. People want me to succeed but they aren't forcing me to be ambitious. I enjoy hard work," he countered unapologetically.

Lilian was sick of serious and ignored his justification. "I like how easy it is to talk to you."

"I like talking to you too. I'm sorry. I understand you need to focus on studying," Jamie conceded, guiltily.

Lilian accepted his apology. "Thank you. I know your impatience comes from a good place."

"I'd better get you home. If you don't ace your exams, you'll never forgive me." Jamie began packing up the picnic before he made any more mistakes.

33

Lilian lay thawing on the concrete as the sun dried her wetsuit. Lactic acid had rendered her muscles useless.

William returned with ice creams from the kiosk.

"Keep moving so you don't stiffen up," William said and passed Lilian her scoop of salted caramel, endeared by the sight of her spent on the ground.

"How can you move? I feel like I might die," Lilian complained. William appeared to have expended no energy.

William crouched next to Lilian and stretched against the bluestone wall separating the boardwalk from the surf beach.

"Don't be so hard on yourself, you were great. It's hard to stand up the first time," William assured her, admiringly.

"For future reference, are there any other extreme sports I should be prepared for when you say it's a surprise?" Lilian croaked. Even her vocal cords hurt.

"Surfing isn't an extreme sport. Do you think fishing is extreme?" William teased.

"I would like to try fishing."

She peeled herself off the pavement and wedged herself between William and the wall.

William had thought Lilian would enjoy surfing and had been impressed by her determination. "Sorry I should have asked you first."

"That's okay. I wouldn't have tried if I didn't want to. I'm having fun, even if you can't have a conversation."

"Are you saying this isn't technically a date if we can't talk? Does that mean we get to have another date before you disappear to study?" William joked.

"No!" Lilian laughed. "I was just making the observation that you can't really get to know someone when you're floating around in the ocean, trying not to drown."

"It sounds like you want a second date, you can just admit it." William grinned.

As Lilian lifted up her arm to playfully punch his thigh, soreness reverberated through her bicep, and she squealed.

"You need to walk it off," William insisted.

Ice cream in one hand, he wrapped his free arm around Lilian and lifted her up. She giggled through the pain as her limbs tingled back to life.

After Lilian had regained her balance, William let go of her waist and they picked up their boards and walked back to the carpark.

"What did you want to talk about?" William asked.

"What do you mean?"

"You wanted to go on a date with conversation. What did you want to know?" William wondered whether there was something on her mind.

"Nothing specific. Sorry I wasn't trying to be critical. This has been a great date. It's nice to do something you like. It feels like most of the time we've spent together has been incidental."

"That's true, but you aren't any less beautiful because you're at work."

"Thanks." Lilian blushed.

Lilian finished her ice cream and William reached comfortably for her hand. "Have you heard back from your interviews yet?"

"Not yet, I'm trying not to think about it," Lilian admitted wearily, the sugar from the ice cream hadn't recharged her yet.

"Are you excited?"

"I'm excited about getting a job. It's the wait I'm not enjoying. How was it for you?"

"I was nervous, for sure. I was hoping to be placed somewhere regional. I've always wanted to experience living in the country before I settle down. Although, I won't be doing much surfing in Bendigo." William laughed.

"There's no surfing in Canberra either," Lilian mumbled.

"What's in Canberra?" William wasn't following.

"Me, maybe. The graduate position with the Tax Office is in Canberra." Lilian hadn't told William she might be leaving Melbourne, she'd been actively avoiding the revelation.

"Oh, I didn't realise. That will be close to home for you," William responded, seemingly unaffected.

"Yes, but not close to you," Lilian noted timidly.

"This has nothing to do with me," William replied, happy for her.

Lilian looked miserable.

"Do you want me to be upset?" William laughed.

"I'd like you to be a little upset," she admitted, hurt by his indifference.

"I'm not upset. It's an amazing opportunity for you and it's going to take more than a five-hour road trip to keep me from you."

Lilian exhaled, relieved, and touched by his resolve.

"You think about settling down?" Lilian asked, revisiting his earlier comment.

"I meant settle down in a specialty at work. My parents want me to take over their clinic eventually, but they know I'm not sure what I want to do yet."

"So marriage and kids are less important than your career?" Lilian deduced. William sounded like he had a plan.

"Not at all. But I'm not thinking about having a family yet. Are you?" William replied, surprised by the inference.

"No, I'm never thinking about that." Lilian laughed, feeling hypocritical.

They arrived at his car.

"I've got something for you." William unlocked the boot and pulled out a black box. "I believe it's your birthday during our study break."

Lilian took the gift. She was sure she hadn't mentioned her birthday.

"It's on the calendar at work," William added, impatient for her reaction.

Lilian lifted the lid. Sitting on a bed of satiny padding was a leather-bound journal. Ignoring the pain, she reached up and kissed his salty cheek. "Thank you. I love it."

34

"Stop laughing." Lilian speared a can with her brand-new rubbish spike.

It was Jane and Lilian's last day as Wilderness Warriors. Vikram and the team had chipped in and bought them both parting gifts.

"I will not." Jane kept laughing defiantly while she retrieved a can from the garden bed bordering the park.

"Guess what? I got both jobs."

Amid the commotion of their surprise departure ceremony, Lilian had forgotten to share her news with Jane.

"Congratulations," Jane screamed and jumped on Lilian, smothering her with kisses. "Both. When? I saw you yesterday."

"The Tax Office called literally a minute after I heard from Bendigo Bank." Lilian gestured for Jane to both clean and talk.

"Which did you pick?" Jane squealed, ignoring Lilian.

"Neither. I don't have the details yet. They were calling me Friday afternoon to tell me they would be emailing me the offer on Monday."

"That's annoying, but still, so exciting," Jane said, finally getting back to work.

"Thanks. I'm so glad I found out before exams. I was worried I'd be stressed the whole time." Lilian tugged on a half-buried bottle.

"Which job sounded better?"

"The Tax Office, but I need to read the contract first. Who knows what kind of wildly unreasonable commitments they expect from graduates?" Lilian's anticipation had not clouded her lawyerly scepticism.

"Are we still pretending Jamie and William don't exist?" Jane said, flouting Lilian's ban on romantic prospects.

"I'll allow it," Lilian joked, curious to hear Jane's thoughts.

"Have you decided which one you want yet?" Jane asked predictably.

"No. As the ban implies, I've not been thinking about either of them," Lilian lied.

"I don't believe you. Do you have a favourite?"

Lilian's first instinct was to deflect, but she was interested in Jane's perspective.

"Lily recommended I think about the life I want, and who is most likely to want the same things. They're both amazing, but the more I get to know them, the more I realise how different my life would be if I ended up with one of them."

"Good point, dump them both. There are probably heaps of equally stunning and accomplished tax lawyers in Canberra," Jane joked.

"That's not what I meant. I like them both. They're just completely different and regardless of the job or the city I feel like I don't know what I want enough to be able to choose yet."

"Yet, you must choose," Jane boomed dramatically.

"Well, I don't have to choose, but I do need to be honest." Lilian laughed. She'd been negotiating with her conscience for a while.

"What does that mean?" Jane asked, confused.

"It means if I can't choose then I need to tell them about each other," Lilian replied, content with her analysis of her introspection.

"How on earth are you going to date them both from Canberra?"

"I don't know. This isn't about which of them I like more. It's about what I want for my life."

"I don't think love works that way. Have you kissed them yet?" Jane asked, unconvinced by Lilian's logic.

"No, I haven't."

"Look, I know you want to be sensible and rational about this, but when you're doing your love maths, can you at least add a vector for sexual attraction. It matters who you want more," Jane pleaded. She was disturbed Lilian was resolute in ignoring the most important consideration.

"Sex is not the only thing that matters, Jane," Lilian snapped, defensively.

"No, Lilian. Sex is the only thing that matters. There are billions of people in the world. You can have all the friends and colleagues and acquaintances you like, but there is only one person you have sex with."

Jane had gotten progressively louder, and was now yelling, drawing concerned looks from families with children clambering on the playground.

"I'm not going to kiss someone as an experiment," Lilian hissed, horrified.

"Say I'm right, Lilian. You know it matters," Jane bit back.

"I'm not saying physical attraction doesn't matter. It's just not the foundation of a lifelong relationship."

"I'm right. I'll take that as a win," Jane claimed smugly.

They arrived at the corner of the park and started working on the adjacent boundary.

Lilian disregarded Jane's prerogative. "Regardless, I've got to choose a job then get through exams. Boyfriends are not my main consideration at the moment."

Jane felt compelled to play devil's advocate. "I know you are determined to make this decision as though Jamie and William don't exist. But they do exist. It's perfectly legitimate to take the one you want into consideration when you decide which job to accept."

Frustrated, Lilian forked a can. "If only it were that simple."

35

Lilian sat with her shoulder pressed against the courtyard wall, staring at a blank page in the journal from William. She was rarely lost for words. Distracted by the faint hum of the traffic, Lilian felt content to enjoy the sounds of Melbourne waking up.

"Happy Birthday, darling." Lily held a long white box secured with a thick gold ribbon.

On birthdays Lilian usually reflected on her plans from the previous year and made new resolutions. Today however she wondered whether rigid goal-setting was obstructing spontaneity from enriching her life.

"Thank you." Lilian dropped her uncapped pen and accepted the present.

"How did you sleep?"

Lilian had posted her signed contract back to the Tax Office then immediately fallen asleep on the couch.

"Well, but I'm still tired." Lilian loosened the ribbon.

"I'm not surprised. It was a big decision, even if you have had your heart set on it for years." Lily left to pour the coffee.

Inside the gift box Lilian found a full-length floral dressing gown. She went to the kitchen to thank Lily.

"Thank you. It's gorgeous. I don't think I have anything this beautiful." Lilian adored the cool smoothness of the silk.

"You're most welcome." Lily smirked, aware Lilian owned nothing even remotely sensual.

"You're not very subtle." Lilian hung the gown over the back of the couch, out of the elements, then carried their mugs back out to the courtyard.

"Darling, when have I ever been subtle?" Lily grinned, taking her seat. "Have you told your boyfriends you'll be leaving Melbourne?"

"No, I won't be seeing either of them until after exams. But they both knew Canberra was my first choice."

"Are you worried?"

The air outside was almost as warm as their drinks.

"William isn't bothered by the distance and I don't know what Jamie thinks."

"Now that you've had some time apart, are you missing one more than the other?"

"No, I'm just focused on exams." Lilian sipped her coffee.

"You know I'm biased. I will be no help," Lily said shamelessly. She was smitten with William.

"Would you like to meet Jamie, so you can make an informed recommendation?" Lilian laughed. She knew Lily would favour them equally.

"No, I would like to remain blissfully unaware, thanks. Unless you want me to?" Lily declared staunchly.

"That's alright. I've been holding back with them both because the other is always in the back of my mind. I don't know if either of them will be forever, but I'd like one of them to be the first."

"That's exciting. Well, you don't have to decide yet. A lot can happen between now and then," Lily speculated ominously.

"Do you know something I don't?" Lilian joked.

"No, darling. I'm just wary of the capricious nature of young romance. I hope they're both where you left them."

"They will be lucky to get a second thought until after exams," Lilian exclaimed. "How's your ankle?"

The bruising had faded to a dull violet and Lily had begun to hobble around the house.

"Not too bad today. No pain yet. It will take longer for my confidence to heal than my leg." Lily glared crossly at the ankle that had betrayed her.

"I don't want to move to Canberra and leave you like this. What if you fall again after I'm gone?" Lilian asked anxiously.

"Do you not have enough to worry about?"

"The only reason I found you when I did was because I came back inside to put Jamie's flowers in the kitchen," Lilian reminded Lily, frustrated her grandmother wouldn't take her own welfare more seriously.

"And if you hadn't been here, I would have crawled to the phone and called someone, and if it had been worse, someone would have realised when I didn't turn up for dinner," Lily rebutted, determined to absolve Lilian of the responsibility she clung to needlessly. "Lilian, I have a daughter to nag me. I don't need a granddaughter to also nag me."

Lilian was upset. "I'm not going to stop worrying about you just because my mother is supposed to worry about you. She lives in a different state."

"I have friends who take care of me, Lilian. Ruth and Doug are my family in Melbourne. They have been looking after me for decades. They're the ones I call when I fall, not Dorothy.

I appreciate you will always worry, but my friends will still be here for me after you're gone." Lily knew she sounded harsh, but it was the truth.

"I know you can take care of yourself. I would just prefer it if there was someone living here with you." Lilian looked at the clock, mindful she needed to start studying.

Lily snapped, sick of Lilian squandering her precious youth. "For goodness' sake. It's your birthday and so far, you've worried about boys, worried about me and worried about exams. Go and have some fun!"

36

Lilian sat under an oak tree and watched students spill out of the exam building.

"We're finished," Jane screamed and leapt on Lilian, knocking them both onto the supple grass.

"My legs feel like jelly," Lilian groaned, unaware when she agreed to go shopping for suits that she would feel so lethargic.

"Are you for real. I feel like I've just had ten coffees." Jane bounced off the ground and pulled Lilian to her feet.

"I need ten coffees." Lilian stretched stiffly.

"Ten coffees it is." Jane did a celebratory dance, then grabbed Lilian's hand and dragged her towards the traffic lights.

"You have to behave yourself. You're wearing a law school jumper." Lilian laughed at the futility of her statement.

Jane had bought them matching jumpers to wear at opposite ends of the world when they missed each other. It was a sweet gesture. Lilian hadn't thought to bring anything for Jane.

"How did you go?" Lilian asked.

"The first essay question was confusing. But I'd like to think Professor Matthews would pass me in my last semester just so she didn't have to teach me again." Jane dreaded the thought of repeating.

"You'll be fine. You worked harder than me this semester," Lilian said, pulling Jane out of the path of a cyclist.

"Let's hope so, because my flights are booked, and I have no home," Jane joked. She had ended her lease. With her family in Adelaide, her graduate position in the Pacific and Lilian moving to Canberra, Jane had no reason to come back to Melbourne. "How'd you go?"

"Good, I think. The questions were really similar to the practice exam."

Jane stopped abruptly and clutched Lilian's shoulders and shouted, "Let's never talk of uni again."

"You can have water tonight," Lilian teased. They were meeting the rest of Professor Matthews' ethics class for karaoke.

"No way. So, when are you seeing Jamie and William again?" Jane asked, determined to pry Lilian out of exam mode.

"You know I haven't spoken to either of them, I've been helping you pack."

The walls in Jane's apartment had been plastered with souvenirs from their adventures and memories from class. It had taken them days to deconstruct.

"I know, we had so much fun. I feel so guilty I won't be here to help you pack for Canberra," Jane sulked.

They stopped at a café for Lilian to refuel.

"I can't believe you're going to be gone this time tomorrow. Can we please enjoy our last day together without wasting time talking about boys I only met a few months ago?"

"To be fair, you've known William your whole life, and you've known Jamie as long as you've known me, but okay. Today is just for us."

Jane left Lilian in the queue and went to the drinks fridge to inspect the selection of flavoured waters.

Lilian felt desperately sad that they'd arrived at their last few hours together.

Jane returned with something recyclable and organic.

"I can't imagine not seeing you every day. I don't even know anyone in Canberra," Lilian said, nervously.

"You'll be fine. You'll have a new best friend by the end of your first day," Jane comforted.

"I will not."

"It's okay, I rescind my title," Jane teased.

Lilian exhaled loudly, overwhelmed by conflicting emotions. "I know things will change. But I can't imagine doing nothing will be this fun with anyone else."

"Life will never be like this again," Jane agreed, finally calming down.

She put her arm around Lilian and mused aimlessly into the distance.

"Now who will stop me from being sensible all the time?" Lilian said.

"I know. Life will be so boring without me." Jane giggled. "I bet there's heaps of sensible people in Canberra for you to be sensible with."

"I certainly hope the Tax Office is full of sensible people." Lilian was horrified by the thought of Jane processing tax returns.

"I'll visit when my posting finishes," Jane promised. "Hopefully you're still the same when I get back."

"Says she who recently admitted she wants to be in a mature relationship," Lilian joked.

Lilian collected her triple-shot iced coffee and they continued toward Bourke Street Mall.

"That's your fault. I have to leave the country to get back to my normal irresponsible self." Jane linked her arm through Lilian's.

"I'm glad some sensibleness finally rubbed off on you or you may not come back in one piece."

Lilian perched her cup on a bollard and pulled out her phone to take a photo of them together in their matching jumpers.

Jane smiled for the picture. "Who knows where we'll end up and isn't that the point!"

37

Lilian met Jamie on the bridge over the Yarra River next to the train station. He had just finished work.

"I feel like I haven't seen you in a year." Jamie pulled Lilian close and squeezed tightly, then stood back and studied her face. "You look relaxed."

As forecast, Jamie had started fulltime work the day after he had finished exams. Barely a breath in between, his transition from university student to professional had transpired as though it were nothing.

"I'm glad I look relaxed because I feel exhausted," Lilian replied.

Crisp and confident in his shirt and loosened tie, Jamie gestured toward the bar. "Did you get the Tax Office job?"

"I did. I'm moving to Canberra," Lilian confirmed.

They entered the island bar and sat side-by-side facing the water. Jamie resisted the urge to confess how much he'd missed her.

"I'm so happy for you," Jamie congratulated appropriately, his heart clenched. "This conversation is going to get bad fast, isn't it?"

"We could pretend I'm not leaving Melbourne until after we've ordered?" Lilian tried unsuccessfully to dispel the tension with a joke.

"Let's do that." Jamie laughed hollowly then put his head in his hands and unleashed a whimpering grunt.

The waiter arrived and frowned concernedly at Jamie. Lilian assured them the faceplanting was theatrical and ordered a jug of non-alcoholic iced tea.

"I want to be clear about this. Please look at me." Lilian slid her hand under his chin and lifted his head.

"Go on, break my heart." Jamie sat up, half smiling, half grimacing.

"Be serious, please," Lilian requested.

Jamie reverted to his normal composed self and took her hand. "Sorry, I'm listening properly."

"I'm moving to Canberra, but I don't want you to look back and think that was the reason we never ended up together. I'm not ready to be in a relationship with you, even if I was staying," Lilian said, then drew a long breath.

"Ouch. Sure, but you're still holding my hand, so I'm a little confused."

"You're amazing. You're so amazing that you're completely certain of what you want, and I feel like there's no room for me," Lilian explained.

"I thought we talked through this at the picnic?" Jamie blurted.

"What I mean is, I don't know what I want for my life yet. But I do know, if I was with you, I would just end up doing whatever you were doing. One day I would wake up and I would have lived your life, not mine."

Jamie considered Lilian's justification. "Sounds like your mind's made up."

He rested his forehead on Lilian's shoulder.

"It's the right decision for both of us." She wrapped her arms around Jamie's neck and hugged him until he was ready to speak.

"Thank you for being honest with me. I would have always wondered what might have been if you'd stayed. I don't want to be in a long-distance relationship, but I would have tried if it meant being with you," Jamie admitted painfully and kissed Lilian's hand.

"I want to say we can be friends, but I don't think I can be your friend." Tears welled in Lilian's eyes.

"I don't want to be friends either," Jamie agreed, hurt in his voice.

"So, this is goodbye for now. Is that okay?" Lilian asked, still in Jamie's arms.

"No," Jamie sulked, "but I understand. Clean break."

The mocktail arrived, forcing an end to their desperate embrace.

"I hope you know how much our time together has meant to me," Lilian said.

"That's a weird thing to say during a break-up." Jamie laughed.

"You know you're a catch," Lilian replied kindly but let go of his hand and shifted away.

"Maybe, if you're lucky, we'll both be single when you get back to Melbourne and you can beg me for a second chance," Jamie joked hopefully.

"There's no way that's going to happen. Carmen will have you married off within a year. You'll be a partner at the firm with a baby by the time I get back."

"You're right, sorry you've missed your chance." Jamie laughed bitterly, then sighed. "Canberra isn't even that far."

"Sorry, this isn't a negotiation." Lilian smiled apologetically.

"I'll miss you," Jamie appealed.

"You know what, I'm going to leave now before you change my mind." Lilian stood up from the bar stool.

Jamie let go of her hand.

"When you look at me like that, I'm glad I went first," Lilian said, holding his stare.

Jamie sighed. "The one debate I needed to win."

38

Lilian waited for William at the jetty. She felt like she might throw up. She had gone to sleep excited to see him again but had woken up full of dread, panicked that he might have changed his mind about her since they went surfing.

William appeared and began to walk down the boardwalk. As he got closer, Lilian registered his wide smile.

"I missed you," William said, pulling her in gently.

"I missed you too." Lilian melted into his chest. "I got the Tax Office job. I'm moving to Canberra."

"I know. Brett told me, Lily told me, Coen told me, and about thirty other people told me." William laughed.

"Of course." Lilian felt guilty, everyone else had still been allowed to talk to her.

"How were your exams?" William asked as they walked toward the beach track.

"Good, I'm so glad I wasn't working. I would have struggled to get through all my notes otherwise."

"Did you find out you got the job before your exams?" William asked. He knew the answer.

"Yes, thankfully, but it took a week to sort out the contract. I start in January."

Now that her exams were over, Lilian was starting to feel

excited about her new job.

"So, we can hang out?" William squeezed her hand.

They took a side path to a secluded lookout.

"I'm so relieved to hear you say that." Lilian sighed.

"Why?" William was bemused.

"I thought you might have gotten over me," Lilian admitted.

"In a few weeks? You're not getting rid of me that easily." William laughed. "I've been busy. I found an apartment and I've been moving my stuff up to Bendigo. Doug's home next week then I'll be heading back up for good."

"Oh, I didn't realise. I thought we'd have more time." Lilian felt intensely disappointed. Inversely, no one had been gossiping to Lilian about William.

He stopped at a clearing and cupped her face.

"This is going to be hard. The distance, trying to see each other. Are you sure it's what you want?"

The wind was blowing the waves against the rocks and a fine sea spray coated them as they held each other.

Lilian searched his face, hoping not to see doubt. "I want this. It doesn't feel hard. It feels like a pace that will last, and that's what I want."

As much as she had missed William, she hadn't minded that they were apart.

"I feel the same, and I'm not in a hurry." William grinned, and they kept walking. "Can I tell people at work you're my girlfriend?"

Lilian felt warmth radiate through her body. "Can I check what that means? I just want to make sure we're on the same page."

"It means I don't want anyone else," William confirmed.

Lilian blushed at her inexperience. "Are you sure? You're about to move to a new city and start a new job."

"So are you." William laughed.

"I just don't want you to make a commitment and then discover there are heaps of people you wish you could date in Bendigo," Lilian said, trying to protect her unscathed heart from future breakage.

When he'd been unpacking in Bendigo, William had realised that he didn't want to be in his apartment with anyone but Lilian.

"I want to be with you. I'm trying to find the sweet spot where you know I'm certain but don't feel pressured." William light-heartedly made a balancing gesture with his hands.

"I'm scared I'll meet someone else. I don't know what will happen," Lilian said, trying to be honest about her fears.

They arrived at the lookout.

"You might meet someone else and, if that happens, I expect you will break up with me and I'm willing to take that risk," William reassured her.

"I hope that doesn't happen."

"How about we worry about breaking up when we get there?" William suggested tenderly.

"Okay," Lilian agreed and closed her eyes as William kissed her hair, content to let the future happen.

39

Lilian had found preparing to move to Canberra unexpectedly confronting. Dorothy had driven down to collect Lilian's mementos for storage in Sydney. William had suggested Lilian keep some essentials in Bendigo. Lily had also insisted Lilian leave her bedroom at the terrace intact for her visits to Melbourne.

Lilian felt her heart being pulled in four directions. Her decisions had further fragmented her already fragmented life.

She packed her journals for safekeeping in Sydney then stared at them anxiously trying to determine whether she would feel incomplete if they were elsewhere. Eventually she decided her most intimate thoughts deserved more respect than to be relegated to a spare cupboard and shifted them to the Canberra pile.

Jane's influence was all over her room. Lilian had designated a box for their memories, which soon overflowed, necessitating a second.

The suits Jane had helped her pick were more sophisticated than Lilian would have chosen alone. She left them hanging in the closet, hoping she would grow into their elegance.

"Do you need some help?" Dorothy asked, passing her a cup of black tea.

Lilian leant against the bedframe. "Thanks. I'm alright, it's just taking forever. I can't remember why I thought half this stuff was important enough to keep."

Dorothy picked up Lilian's High School Graduation photo from the top of the Sydney pile and found Lilian in the line-up.

"I can't believe how much you've grown." Dorothy noticed her daughter's bright hopeful eyes in the photo. She was grateful Lilian had managed to retain enthusiasm after losing her father so young.

"I think I look the same. What did you think of William?" Lilian asked.

Feeling left out, Dorothy had wanted to meet her daughter's new boyfriend. So William had cooked dinner for Dorothy at the terrace.

"He's charming," Dorothy commented.

It had been enlightening to watch William and Lilian cooking together. They had been relaxed, happy to be in each other's company, the kind of easiness which was completely foreign to Dorothy. Her relationships had always started frenzied and heated.

"He's pretty great," Lilian agreed, enamoured. "Do you mind if I stay in Bendigo with William until Christmas Eve?"

"Sure, I'm planning on bringing the twins down to Melbourne that week. Marcus wants to see Lily, I think he got a fright when she fell. They're coming around to the idea of me moving back."

Dorothy returned the photo and walked over to the window above the courtyard. She admired Lilian's green oasis below. "All those plants are going to die when you leave."

"Lily has arranged for Ruth's granddaughter to take care of

my garden. Apparently she's studying landscape design." Lilian finished her tea and got back to sorting.

"We're going shopping for graduation outfits this afternoon. Would you like to come?" Dorothy offered, glancing doubtfully at the unsorted mounds.

"I don't have time, but thanks though. I have to finish packing today."

"Are you ready for the ceremony?" Dorothy asked with a raised eyebrow.

"Do you mean am I worried William will run into Jamie?" Lilian laughed.

She had been allocated three guest tickets and had invited Dorothy, Lily and William.

"I didn't, but are you?"

"Not at all. I told William about Jamie. He's like me, very rational."

"Love isn't rational, nor is jealously," Dorothy said.

"Perhaps, but William trusts me," Lilian dismissed.

"Well, that's good, given you're going to be living in different cities. And do you trust him?"

"Yes. He wouldn't be with me if he didn't want to be," Lilian justified confidently. She had told William about the curse. William had dismissed Lilian's forewarning as nonsense.

"You clearly don't need a mother," Dorothy joked, feeling thoroughly unrequired by her utterly capable daughter.

Lilian couldn't concentrate, so she joined Dorothy on the bed.

"Maybe, but I want one," she replied. "I hope you don't move to Melbourne too soon. I was looking forward to seeing you all again on weekends."

"I would love that, but don't worry if you can't get back to see us. You have your own life now. Families grow apart, people leave to make their own families," Dorothy said, remembering leaving Lily. "You two might decide to stay in Bendigo or Canberra, who knows?"

"Jane would never forgive me if I didn't come back to Melbourne," Lilian said nudging the boxes dedicated to their friendship.

"Jane will find a partner and you'll both make new friends. That's just life. People move around, and apart."

"I know, but she's such an enormous part of my life. It's hard to imagine." Lilian refused to believe their bond could break.

"Life is an adventure. You grow and change with each challenge. I'm not the same as I was in my twenties, and nor would I want to be," Dorothy comforted.

Grateful for the reassurance, Lilian got back to packing up her past to make way for her future. "See, I do need a mother."

40

William would be arriving soon. Lilian had stripped her bed, put the sheets in the washing machine and cleaned her bathroom. Once she'd finished vacating the upper floor, Lilian tiptoed down the stairs and settled in the courtyard to complete her last journal entry.

Lilian hadn't reflected on finishing her law degree until her graduation ceremony. After listening to the speakers describe the obligation that accompanied the vesting of knowledge, the significance of her achievement had resonated.

Lilian had asked William to film Lily and Dorothy as she walked across the stage. She wanted him to capture their reactions. Loss had taught her that these moments with her family were fleeting and precious.

Brett had organised a party at the Marina to celebrate Lilian's departure. She had thought by then she would have been exhausted, but with each day, each decision made, she felt lighter. Originally daunted by the thought of leaving, Lilian had realised the Marina's rhythm now felt predictable and she knew she was ready to move on.

Lilian finished documenting the era about to end and rebound her journal. She rested her shoulder against the warm bricks and listened to the traffic. The flowers had died back in the heat and the air was sticky, heavy with humidity. She wouldn't be breathing salty sea air anytime soon.

Lily appeared, tearing up already. "Morning, darling. When's William picking you up?"

"Any minute. Coffee? I made a pot." Lilian didn't think Lily would be up in time to say goodbye and had made the coffee herself.

"No journal?" Lily asked, noticing Lilian wasn't writing.

"I've decided to take a break. Live my life instead of writing about it."

"Is that what you've been doing this whole time?" Lily smiled.

"No, just overthinking." Her journals had saved her, but she had outgrown them.

"You may have more important things to do in the mornings," Lily teased. "Are you all packed?"

"Everything's ready, my bags are by the front door," Lilian confirmed. She'd checked and double checked.

"I'm going to miss you," Lily said then burst into tears.

Lilian went to hug her grandmother, feeling the familiar fear that it may be the last time. "I will miss you every day."

"Dorothy wants me to visit for the summer, so I'll see you in Sydney for Christmas," Lily assured her.

Lily usually spent holidays at the Marina, but this year she craved her family.

"That's great. Everyone together in one place, finally." Lilian sighed, relieved it wouldn't be long until they saw each other again.

The doorbell rang and Lilian sprang up. "I'll pack the car then come back in to say goodbye."

Lilian raced down the hallway and opened the door.

"Hi, you ready?" William kissed her cheek.

"Yes," Lilian said excitedly and lifted one of her cases.

William carried the rest of the luggage to the boot.

Lily stood at the library window and watched Lilian collect the last of her bags.

"Is Lily up?" William had double parked.

"Yes, do you mind circling the block while I say goodbye?"

"Sure, take your time," William shouted as a car drove up behind him, then he sped away.

Lilian ran back inside and hugged Lily tightly. "It's time. Thank you for taking such good care of me."

Lily thought back to the nervous, timid teenager who had arrived on her doorstep, and how grateful she was to have witnessed her grow into the smiling self-assured woman leaving today.

"It was my absolute pleasure," Lily said, overwhelmed with love and sadness.

"Bye, I'll see you at Christmas," Lilian promised, letting go of her grandmother.

William pulled up and Lilian jumped in the front seat.

"I love you," Lillian yelled through the open window.

"Bye. Have fun. I love you too," Lily called back.

William waved as they slowly pulled away.

Lilian wiped her tears.

"Are you alright?" William asked, taking her hand.

Lilian watched the terrace fade in the rear-view mirror. Overcome with emotion, she decided to look forward and not back, then focused on the road ahead. "Yes, I just love her. A lot!"

41

Lilian could hear William in the shower. Her heart sank when she noticed his case resting against the kitchen bench. Another weekend without her husband.

Lilian tossed her car keys in the fruit bowl and began clearing the breakfast dishes.

William emerged in a towel and blew her a kiss on his way to their bedroom.

The home phone rang.

"How about a hot air balloon ride?" Lilian's step-grandfather blurted.

"Morning, Al. Sounds dangerous?" Lilian said, rebuffing the suggestion.

Al murmured to himself, considering the risks.

Lilian adored Al's efforts to romance Lily, and his delight at involving the entire family in the process.

"Perhaps something more grounded?" Lilian nudged while cramming utensils into the dishwasher.

The excitement of celebrating their five-year wedding anniversary had inflamed Al's grandiose desire to honour his wife. Lilian and Ari had fortunately intercepted and quashed his outlandish ideas thus far.

"Alright." Al grunted in defeat then hung up.

Short bursts of Al were the norm. Lilian smiled to herself and replaced the handset.

William returned, radiant from his morning surf, wearing a curious expression. No one rang the home phone anymore.

"Al, more anniversary ideas," Lilian explained.

"Sky diving?" William joked.

"Close, hot air ballooning." Lilian laughed performatively. Her husband was about to disappear again.

William saw her disappointment and whisked her away from the chores.

"I'm sorry." He wrapped Lilian in his arms and kissed her neck.

Tom had been a mess after Maggie died and, a year on, William was still leaving Sydney every few weekends to care for his father in Melbourne.

"You don't have to apologise." Lilian kissed him back. "We just miss you while you're away."

"No buts?" William pressed, his guilt compounded with every trip.

"None," Lilian lied.

It was an unwinnable argument. His mother had died horridly and William was still grieving. During her last days Maggie had reflected on the irony that, of all the lives she'd saved, she couldn't save her own. Tom echoed her pain. A family full of doctors and no one had realised Maggie was sick until there was nothing that could be done. Weekends with Tom provided William some comfort.

William ran his hands under her loose linen shirt.

Lilian, succumbing, opened one eye and glanced over at the clock.

"We don't have time."

He reluctantly followed her gaze. "We've got heaps of time."

William pulled out his phone and presented his boarding pass. Lilian had already seen the printout sitting on top of his luggage.

"The flight doesn't board at quarter past, it departs at quarter past," Lilian corrected.

William examined the ticket, realised his error, shrugged, and kept kissing her.

"Go." Lilian laughed, removing herself from his embrace.

William groaned and collected his wallet and keys from the fruit bowl.

"We'll finish this conversation when I get back." He snuck one last kiss.

Tingling with bittersweetness, Lilian sighed and focused on gratitude until the sensation passed, then continued cleaning the kitchen.

As Lilian was wiping the last of the crumbs from the benchtop, the home phone chimed again.

"Darling, how are you?" Lily asked curtly.

Lilian removed her rubber gloves and slumped against the bench, tempted to be honest about her sore heart.

"Hi, Lily, I'm well. How are you?" she replied, doubting Lily was calling about her.

"Have you spoken to Al? He's been very secretive this week. I'm worried he's planning something ridiculous for our anniversary?"

Lily viewed her marriage as a strategic victory. Having refused to leave the terrace to move into Al's retirement village, Lily suggested they get married instead. Al agreed on the condition Lily spent weekends with him. Lily's part-time husband suited her, except when he was plotting in her absence.

"I decline to comment on the grounds I may incriminate myself," Lilian teased.

"I knew it!" Lily exclaimed. "What's he planning?"

"I can't tell you. But I can divulge it will be on land," Lilian confirmed cryptically.

"Oh, you two and your scheming," Lily snapped and hung up the phone.

Lilian dialled Lily's number.

"Darling, I forgive you," Lily answered. "Now I must go, I have bridge. Will I see you soon?"

Lilian scoured the family calendar hanging next to the fridge. There were more birthday parties than days.

"I am very old, Lilian," Lily scolded.

She didn't need reminding. "Soon, Lily. I hope soon."

42

Lilian arrived late to find her colleagues eavesdropping on their boss.

Murph, Mala and Yael were pressed against the internal partition with the reception lobby. Muhammad, partaking via his intercom, greeted Lilian with a gleeful wave.

Intrigued, Lilian crossed the open plan office and dialled in from her desk.

"So you want me to agree to be insulted?" the new client said.

"As I explained, Mr Clarker, you will not necessarily be insulted. Also, this is not an agreement, it is a condition of working with Bondi Singh Tax Excellence. It's your choice whether to proceed with us." Clarise reeled off her standard script.

"Can you give me an example?" Mr Clarker grumbled.

Clarise masterfully concealed her impatience. "If one were somewhat rotund, one's appearance may be commented upon, tactlessly."

Murph flung both hands over his mouth to suppress a howl.

Mr Clarker pondered the comment, certain he had just been insulted. "I am a businessman, Mrs Yun. I am of the mind there is a strong correlation between good service and manners."

Clarise replied sternly.

"Mr Clarker, we are a neurodiverse practice. Our staff are perfectly capable of conforming to the bounds of polite society.

Jason and I prefer they vest their superior intellects in their work." Clarise tapped the last word on the sign behind her. "This is how we achieve excellence."

Partially convinced, Mr Clarker scowled at the contract clamped between his pudgy fingers.

"I see there are other requirements. I will take some time to digest the terms and ensure we are able to comply before signing." Mr Clarker stood to leave and lent forward and shook Clarise's hand.

"Please take your time, Mr Clarker. No aftershave or strong scents and you should be fine." Clarise refrained from adding no handshakes.

"My associates speak highly of your advice, Mrs Yun. I'm sure we will be able to find a workable solution." Mr Clarker looked down at his portly belly and sighed. "I will prepare to be told I am a very fat man."

Clarise opened the foyer door.

Lilian and Muhammed skimmed their correspondence while the others scurried back their desks.

"Get back to work," Clarise said, shaking her head at the spies as she passed.

"I have been working the whole time." Muhammed grinned.

"Sure you have. If Mr Clarker comes back, Mala, you will need to provide preliminary advice within a week. Lilian, join me for tea," Clarise instructed then strode off.

Lilian collected her mug from its coaster home and followed Clarise to the kitchen.

"Close the door please." Clarise plucked a fancy tea bag from her personal stash. "Would you like to try this lemongrass and ginger blend?"

Unable to read Clarise's monotone, Lilian erred on the side of being agreeable. "I'd love to."

Lilian filled her cup with boiling water then sat opposite Clarise at the homely table.

"I know you have a lot to get through today, so I will get straight to the point," Clarise began.

Lilian smiled. Clarise had no other speed.

"Jason and I had our directors' meeting this week, and we are concerned you're wasted here."

Lilian laughed, she was expecting a rebuke over her lateness. "I'm not sure what to make of that."

"Well, you started working here as a favour to me and then you never left." Clarise slumped guiltily against the back of her wooden chair. She blamed herself for derailing Lilian's career.

Feeling ambushed, Lilian took a moment to compose herself.

Clarise was right. Clarise had been complaining she couldn't find suitably qualified staff while they had been waiting together for their daughters to finish ballet class. Lilian had offered to help a few hours a week while she was at home raising her girls. Now years later, Lilian had inadvertently morphed into a fulltime pseudo-director.

"Where are you going with this?" Lilian asked bluntly.

"All I meant to say was, if you want to stay, then we'd love you to stay. But let's talk about your role here and whether you want your name on the door," Clarise clarified, embarrassed it had taken her so long to initiate the conversation.

"Thank you, I'll have to think about it," Lilian managed, less than flattered.

"Please take all the time you need. This isn't an ultimatum, honestly, I just didn't think you'd still be here," Clarise admitted.

The offer was meant to be a compliment, but instead the expectation stung. Lilian picked up her luxurious tea and returned to her desk. She didn't know where Clarise thought she should have gone by now, but the implication was, anywhere but Bondi Singh Tax Excellence.

43

Dot was trying not to laugh at her Uncle Carlos dressed as a clown, juggling and performing for her cousin's birthday party. His delighted daughters squealed and bounced on the floor, surrounded by friends and fluffy toys.

"They're adorable," Lilian whispered to Ari.

"They have no idea what he's doing." Ari watched her transfixed twin two-year-olds stare at their father adoringly. "Beth on the other hand looks very worried."

"Magic freaks her out," Lilian explained on behalf of her youngest daughter.

Carlos' disappearing thumb had Beth clutching Jordan, who had refused to join his father in a matching clown outfit. As a compromise, Jordan had worn a Batman mask styled with a Superman cape.

"Mum not here?" Lilian asked.

"No, she couldn't get a flight this morning. It was Juan's birthday yesterday, they were out partying." Ari chastised their mother like she was a misbehaving teen.

"Why didn't she just bring Juan to the party?"

"She doesn't want him to know she's a grandmother," Ari conveyed, appalled.

"What!" Lilian exclaimed louder than she had intended,

momentarily distracting Beth from the tricks. "She's got five grandchildren. Where's she planning on hiding them?"

"I did point that out. I said that if Juan doesn't love her as she is with four kids and five grandkids, then she shouldn't be with him."

"Deception is antithetical to her entire business philosophy," Lilian commented, sounding judgemental.

"Mum says her decision not to disclose she's a mother or a grandmother is empowering and forces Juan to see her as a woman, and that it's her choice not to cloud the relationship with unnecessary details," Ari repeated, with a mix of repulsion and amusement.

Ari had taken over managing Dorothy's business in Sydney when Dorothy had moved to Melbourne to take care of Lily. Dorothy still helped when Ari needed support, which was most days. As a result, Lilian usually heard her mothers' anecdotes second-hand from her sister.

"That's ludicrous." Lilian laughed in disbelief.

"When I call her I say, 'Mum, it's the details calling'. She doesn't think it's very funny."

"Why doesn't she want him to know about us?" Lilian wondered aloud, sceptical of Ari's version of events.

Lily had told her a few months ago that Dorothy had taken a lover. Lilian had assumed Lily was being sensational.

"I don't know, but the double-life is starting to get annoying." Ari's complaint was cut short when Carlos began a chorus of Happy Birthday.

Ari rushed to help Jordan manoeuvre the giant ice cream cake through the blanket of toddlers crammed into their tiny apartment.

After the candles were safely extinguished, Dot began helping Jordan de-costume.

Beth, relieved the show was over, retreated to the safety of Lilian's lap.

"Did you have fun?" Lilian asked doubtfully.

"Yes," Beth lied.

Lilian looked down at her tired little face. Beth never slept well on the weekends William was away. "Do you want to play with Connie and Abbie while everyone finishes their cake, and then we can go home?"

"Alright." Beth agreeably joined her cousins on the floor and showed them how to build a wall with Duplo blocks.

"No William?" Carlos asked, plonking himself next to Lilian on the couch.

"William's with Tom this weekend."

"All good. I will photoshop him into the pictures," Carlos said while eating a melting blob of ice cream cake with his fingers.

"Would you like a spoon?" Lilian offered.

"No, it tastes better if you eat it in a fun way," Carlos replied matter-of-factly.

Carlos was endlessly silly. It was part of why Ari fell in love with him. Ari was naturally flighty, and Carlos was freshly entertaining every day.

Lilian passed her brother-in-law a stack of napkins. "Your house, your rules."

Guests were starting to leave, and they watched Ari hand out party bags and distribute balloons.

"How are rehearsals going?"

"Well, very well. We have a new conductor and she's pushing us so hard, it's so inspiring. We didn't even know we'd become stale. You know?" Carlos spoke about his work like it was an addiction and treated everyone like they understood the inner-workings of an orchestra.

Lilian had never played an instrument, but she was feeling stale herself.

"You are already exceptional. It must have been exciting to discover you have another level?"

"That's exactly how it felt. Like she came in, swept us off our feet, and lifted us up to another level."

Carlos emitted positive energy whenever he spoke about music. He was like a radiator.

Abbie threw a Duplo brick at Connie, sparking tears on both sides.

Carlos licked the last of his liquid cake from the bowl and got up to attend to his worn out daughters. "Lovely to have a grown-up chat with you, Sis."

44

"I don't want Daddy to leave anymore," Dot cried, rubbing her eyes. Lilian sat on the edge of Dot's bed. She didn't want William to leave either.

"I know, but we need to share Daddy with Grandpa Tom for a little while because he misses Grandma Maggie," Lilian replied diplomatically.

"How much longer?" Dot huffed between sobs.

After an exhausting few days, it was a fair question. William had called Sunday afternoon to tell Lilian he needed to stay in Melbourne another night and would explain why when he got back. In the absence of a comprehendible reason their father had not come home, the girls had become extremely anxious. When William arrived Monday night, he'd played with them both well past their bedtime, but the shock of the betrayal remained. They had lost faith.

"Would you like to have an adventure with Daddy and visit Grandpa Tom?" Lilian tried to salvage the arrangement.

Dot stared at her clenched hands. "I just want Daddy to stay here."

Dot's rejection was unsurprising. She barely knew her grandparents, they were all in Melbourne.

"Have a think about it." Lilian kissed her cheek and turned off the lamp.

Beth was already asleep, preceded by a similar conversation. Neither of their daughters were falling for the consolation of a fun weekend away with Dad.

Lilian found William unpacking in their bedroom. She sat in the bay window reading nook.

Lilian had been so busy with the girls and work she hadn't even bothered worrying about the reason her husband had absconded.

"You're annoyed," William commented, watching her nestle into the cushions.

"I'm not annoyed, I'm just waiting for you to tell me why you didn't come home." Lilian was impressed by how evenly she spoke, when what she felt was abandoned.

"Sorry, I didn't mean to sound so dramatic when I called. I was in the kitchen with Dad so I couldn't talk," William apologised.

Uncomfortable, Lilian got up from the nook and moved to the bed.

"Shirley called and asked me to meet with the staff. You know Shirley, she'd never ask unless it was serious."

Lilian nodded in agreement. Shirley had been the receptionist at Tom and Maggie's medical clinic since before William had been born. Shirley was considered family and was Tom's best friend, although he'd never admit it.

"I went to the meeting and listened to the staff. Shirley wanted me to hear from the other doctors that Dad's slipping. He's been making mistakes and they've been covering for him, but they're scared he's going to miss something."

"Why don't they talk to Tom about this?" Lilian masked her irritation. It seemed like an extreme escalation to call his son in from interstate.

"They're worried about his mental health. They're scared that if he retired he wouldn't have anything to live for," William shared sadly.

Lilian and William had had the same concerns when they decided William should continue to visit Tom on weekends.

"Anyway, they don't want him to leave, they just want someone to take over. They asked me to come back and run the Clinic," William added as he zipped up his suitcase and hauled it back onto the top shelf of the closet.

"You're a surgeon," Lilian blurted before she could restrain herself.

"Yes, but my parents have been telling people I will be taking over the Clinic since I went to medical school. Everyone assumes one day we will go back to Melbourne." William picked up the full washing basket to take to the laundry. "The other doctors are just thinking about their futures, and they want to protect Dad. Back in a sec."

Lilian waited, baffled by the misguided perceptions of people so close to Tom.

William returned with two glasses of water and joined her on the bed.

"So how did the meeting end?"

"I told them I'd talk to Dad."

"What does that mean?" Lilian twinged at the vagueness, annoyed he didn't tell them to talk to Tom themselves.

"I agree with them. I don't want him to leave the Clinic. He's too miserable to find something productive to do if he retires now. Sticking to his routine has kept him going."

"You aren't responsible for any of this," Lilian said, angry at the cowards for dragging William into their problems.

"Maybe, but nonetheless, I am," William said gently. He took Lilian's hand and kissed it.

Lilian had spent hours trying to convince their daughters that they were their fathers' priority, and nothing would keep him away from them. Now Lilian was wondering whether her husband was about to make her a liar.

"Did you tell Shirley your daughters need you in Sydney and you aren't coming back to run the Clinic?"

William sighed sheepishly. "I told her I'd think about it."

45

"I'm not married, but I'm pretty sure you have to be trying not to tell your husband you got a promotion," Rachel teased.

"Well, whose fault is that?" Lilian deflected.

Charlie had asked Rachel to marry her monthly since they had moved in together. Rachel had no interest in joining the institution.

"Don't make this about me." Rachel laughed.

"Honestly, William was in Melbourne and when he got home he was worried about Tom and I completely forgot," Lilian insisted above the applause.

"Do you want to stay at Bondi Singh?" Rachel asked, not persuaded by Lilian's supposed memory lapse.

"I assumed I would eventually go back to the Tax Office," Lilian fibbed. She'd never thought about it. "Anyway, we don't have time to talk about this, your category is up next."

Rachel's most recent book on managing finances for young women had been a bestseller and her publisher had nominated her for Businesswoman of the Year. Unexpectedly, the council had shortlisted Rachel alongside actual businesswomen who ran local businesses.

"You mean our category," Rachel corrected.

Lilian had been surprised that Rachel had named her as a co-author, as Lilian had barely done any of the work.

"I want you to write another book with me," Rachel suggested whimsically.

"You're already writing another book, you don't need me," Lilian reminded Rachel.

The audience chatted amongst themselves while the presenter handed out achievement awards.

"I'm just putting the offer on the table," Rachel said, patting the starched tablecloth.

Even though Rachel was a non-fiction superstar, she was loath to admit the journey had been terribly lonely.

"Pretending to co-author one book is quite enough fraud for me, thank you," Lilian replied cheekily.

"You wrote a whole chapter. You're fully deserving of your named author status."

Rachel didn't mind sharing the spotlight, she relished the camaraderie.

The presenter arrived at Rachel's category. She had been forewarned she would be the winner.

"You're very kind," Lilian said, accepting the gracious praise from her old friend.

"I am, and you're stalling." Rachel grinned. "When are you going to tell William that Clarise offered you a directorship?"

Lilian hadn't been completely truthful with Rachel. The conversation with Clarise hadn't slipped her mind, it was stuck in her mind. She didn't want to talk to William until she knew what she wanted.

"Soon. Clarise implied I should be working somewhere prestigious…" Lilian's reply was cut short by an usher who had arrived to collect Rachel.

"Hold that thought," Rachel said.

As the presenter introduced the finalists Lilian felt a familiar uneasiness return, the same queasy sensation that had plagued her throughout high school.

The Mayor announced Rachel had won and passed her a small trophy. Rachel glowed. She was genuinely as impressive as her achievements.

Once the cheer subsided, Rachel was invited to address her fans.

"Thank you to the Councillors for bestowing me with this honour. My fellow nominees are truly remarkable, I'm shocked to have been selected as the winner in this distinguished company." Rachel led applause from the crowd for the worthy women who had missed out.

"I would like to thank my dear co-author, Lilian, who is here with me tonight. We have been best friends since she stole my boyfriend at uni, and it was a pleasure to write alongside such a talented and generous tax lawyer." Rachel raised her trophy to Lilian who stood and waved at the guests now staring at her.

The fact that Lilian had never even kissed Jamie didn't get in the way of Rachel's joyfully concocted anecdote. Charlie did not appreciate Rachel's quip that Jamie was the one that got away.

"We are so grateful our book has been able to reach so many young women and encourage them to take control of their financial futures. It's a blessing to be able to work alongside people you love, and Council's acknowledgement of our contribution to this community is icing on the cake."

Lilian was moved. Rachel was too modest. Her work really was transformational, and she deserved the recognition for her books which had enriched so many women.

Rachel plonked her trophy on the table. "That thing is deceptively heavy."

"Beautiful speech." Lilian hugged Rachel while others on their table queued to shake her hand.

"Thank you," Rachel repeated, accepting their praise.

Their celebration was curtailed by coffee and cake.

Rachel relaxed, relieved the formalities were over. "Sorry we were interrupted. Why did Clarise offer you a promotion out of nowhere?"

"She believes she ruined my career. I think it was a consolation offer," Lilian guessed.

"Poor Clarise. You hated the Tax Office, and you were bored out of your mind on maternity leave. Fortunately, I saved you with my book. Did you tell her you stay because you're happy?" Rachel inquired, trying to ignore her admirers hovering nearby.

"I always wanted to be a lawyer and I'm a lawyer. The girls are my priority now and work is just work."

"Was that Clarise's point," Rachel suggested.

Lilian was embarrassed she didn't have a thoroughly considered reply. Her accomplished friend would never be so ambivalent about her own decisions.

Rachel's trophy twinkled under the lights.

Lilian winced. "I don't know, I need to think about it."

46

Dot and Jordan knelt under the front window of the ferry, entertained by the exploding spray of the waves crashing against the bow. Beth, wedged between them, was distracted by a crew of unruly teens running up and down the aisles.

Lilian and Ari watched their children from a nearby table. Dorothy and Lily sat opposite, clutching steaming takeaway cups for warmth.

The conversation had been halted when their phones chimed in unison. Carlos had sent another group message with a photo of the twins watching cartoons.

"Cute?" Dorothy questioned, confused by the sharing of an apparently unremarkable moment.

Ari mimicked a shot to her heart.

"Don't give me that, your grandmother is trying to tell us a story."

"Thank you, darling. As I was saying, after we had high tea we went to the symphony and then out to dinner. It was spectacular," Lily gushed.

"Congratulations," Lilian raised her thermos to toast the epic anniversary.

Lily wasn't finished boasting. "Can you believe Al arranged for the conductor to play my favourite score, and he planned the whole menu. All seven courses."

Lilian tried to remember when she'd last been on a date with William. She couldn't recall.

"Thank you for helping Al. He loves an excuse to speak to you." Lily patted Lilian's hand.

Lilian smiled, satisfied with the outcome of her interventions. Unbeknown to Lily, she had almost ended up on an outback safari.

"Any wildly romantic stories you would like to share?" Ari said to Dorothy.

Dorothy, stone-faced, was unimpressed by the intrusion. "Nothing I can think of."

"Doesn't your mother's skin look buoyant? Being in love is doing wonders for your complexion," Lily remarked.

Ari and Lilian sniggered. No one could get away with speaking to Dorothy like that, except Lily.

Ari opened her mouth to say something snarky and Dorothy interrupted.

"Ari is upset because I haven't told Juan about the family," Dorothy explained to Lily.

"I know, darling." Lily glanced compassionately at her daughter.

"I'm not upset. I'm offended you wish your granddaughters didn't exist," Ari blurted, holding up the mundane photo of her toddlers laying on throw cushions.

"It's extraordinary how you manage to make everything about you," Dorothy snapped back loudly.

"Boat voices please," Lily interjected.

"How is this not about us? You're embarrassed by us," Ari hissed.

Lilian kept her eyes on their children, avoiding being drawn into the conflict.

Dorothy realised the hurt she'd inadvertently caused was unfair and her frustration turned to guilt. "I'm sorry I didn't explain myself better."

"Well then try." Ari huffed and crossed her arms, waiting for the impending excuse.

"It's not that I don't want Juan to know about you. I'm just delaying telling him I'm a widow."

"Why do you care if he knows you're a widow?" Ari asked confused.

Lily and Dorothy shared a knowing glance.

"Because when people find out you're a widow, they treat you differently. Eric died so long ago, I'm sick of the pity. Juan knows me as a fierce independent woman. I don't want him to see me any other way."

Ari blushed, ashamed she'd assumed her mother was being callous. "Sorry, I didn't realise."

Their phones erupted with another photo of the twins, now eating, bibs and faces covered in jam. Carlos also covered in jam.

Beth had left her perch and was swaying slowly toward the table.

Lilian prepared to catch her upon arrival.

"They're going to fall over," Beth whispered to Lilian, still monitoring the daredevils.

Lilian looked down at her pensive daughter, always so concerned for others.

"They know they might fall over, they're just having fun," Lilian explained.

"Falling over isn't fun," Beth disputed.

"No, it isn't," Lilian agreed. "Do you want to stay here or sit with Dot?"

Beth took a deep breath, stressed by the recklessness of others, and determinedly began the fraught trip back to the window.

Relieved her sister and mother had reconciled, Lilian rejoined the adults.

"You were exactly the same at that age," Dorothy said, having eavesdropped on her daughter's parenting.

"I have no doubt." Lilian smiled.

Beth clutched Dot victoriously.

"Sometimes I wonder why I'm still in Melbourne. I'm missing so much."

"Lily needs you," Lilian absolved.

Lily was on the phone, flirting shamelessly with Al.

"She's going to live for another twenty years," Dorothy joked.

Loving Al had rejuvenated Lily, but she had nonetheless become frail. They all knew Lily didn't have long.

"Are you planning on coming back to Sydney?" Lilian winked.

"I'm not in love with Juan, we just appreciate each other's company," Dorothy said, dismissing her inference.

"For now."

Dorothy ignored the comment.

"Is everything alright at home?" Dorothy asked Ari.

"Yes, the jam disaster was staged." Ari laughed. Typical Carlos, always the performer.

The unnerving youths had grown bored of the aisles and returned to their families, enabling Beth to join Dot and Jordan in wave gazing.

"I was just saying, I'm missing out on their childhoods," Dorothy repeated for Ari.

It was a rhetorical comment. Dorothy wanted to spend whatever time she had left with Lily, but it came at a cost.

"Mum, they don't know any different," Ari offered kindly.

"No, but I miss them," Dorothy replied.

Lily giddily ended her call. "Al sends his love. He's already trying to plan my eightieth."

Lilian laughed, dreading the thought, and drained her tea ready to disembark.

"I told him to butt out," Lily assured them. "My birthday, my party."

47

Light reflected off Sydney Harbour causing blinding sunbeams to bounce around the shiny white boardroom. Lilian looked down at the Opera House then stepped back from the window, the immediate drop to the street was making her dizzy.

She sat with her back to the brightness outside. Through a glazed internal wall, a woman waved at Lilian while she approached.

"Lilian, sorry to have kept you waiting. I'm Maddison. Thanks for coming into our office. It's a tad challenging for me to get to Bondi in the middle of the day," Maddison said warmly, oblivious to the offensiveness of her comment.

"Nice to meet you," Lilian replied, leaning over the enormous table to shake Maddison's outstretched hand.

"I apologise for being cagey about our project. It took some convincing for your boss to agree to the meeting without me signing your special agreement." Maddison clasped Lilian's hand with both of hers.

Lilian waited for Maddison to say something substantial.

"My assistant will be here shortly to take minutes. In the meantime, tell me about yourself."

Lilian wasn't sure whether Maddison wanted to hear about her work or her family.

"I'm a tax lawyer. I used to work at the Australian Tax Office. I live in Bondi with my husband, William, he's a surgeon, and our two girls, Beth and Dot." Lilian examined Maddison's expression, hoping her life summary was on point.

Maddison lurched forward and clapped with delight. "Dot, what a lovely name. You never hear that anymore."

"Dot is short for Dorothy. Dot is named after my mother. It's a family tradition, I was named after my grandmother," Lilian offered, starting to feel like she had ambled into a sitcom.

"So beautiful. And what do you do for fun?" Maddison probed, twisting to eyeball her assistant who then began running up the hallway.

"I…" Lilian started, then the assistant burst through the door.

"Sorry I'm late." He bowed his apology to Maddison.

"Lilian, this is Dion," Maddison said dismissively then powered up her tablet.

"Nice to meet you, Dion," Lilian replied.

Dion ignored the acknowledgment and shrunk into the background.

"Lilian, what has Clarise told you?" Maddison checked, seemingly done with the filler fun question.

"Unfortunately, I haven't had a chance to speak with Clarise. Perhaps you could start from the start, if it isn't too much trouble?" Lilian scrambled, she didn't want to embarrass Clarise.

"Not at all, Lilian. I'd prefer to explain our proposal in full." Lilian smiled. *Phew*, she thought.

"I did read your contract, Bondi Singh is quite unique."

"Our practice is neurodiverse," Lilian corrected.

"Fair enough." Maddison momentarily reflected on the explanation. "Well, we won't be signing it because we can't comply, but I do hope that we can come to an alternative agreement."

Lilian was taken aback. Clarise would not have consented to the meeting knowing their terms of service were not amenable.

"In that case, I'm not sure why I'm here," Lilian replied truthfully.

"Apologies, Lilian. I've not been clear. I approached Clarise because I wanted to hire you, not your company. I was hoping you would consider taking on our firm as a client, personally," Maddison revealed.

"Who recommended me?" Lilian asked sceptically.

"It was your director in Canberra. We're family friends. I mentioned I needed an expert in tax law, specifically deductions. Henrietta said you were her best."

Lilian had been fond of Henrietta. Apparently Henrietta had given up hope Lilian would return to the Tax Office.

"So this is a job interview?" Lilian questioned.

Maddison pursed her glossy lips.

"We would like to engage you to provide expert advice to our management team. Our in-house lawyers and accountants can handle the Tax Office. It's when the Commissioner starts refusing my deductions that we need someone more specialised."

Lilian had become nauseated by the reflected harbour water combined with the disingenuous invitation, but resisted the urge to excuse herself.

"If you don't want to sign our agreement to work with Bondi Singh, how are you expecting to be able to work with me?"

"It's my understanding that contract relates to clients attending your office. We would need you to work here fulltime, like a secondment."

Lilian ignored the insulting presumption she would agree to make a daily trip Maddison couldn't manage once. "What are you doing that's causing the Commissioner to refuse your deductions?"

"We sell domestic violence insurance." Maddison produced her first sincere smile of the meeting.

"I've never heard of such an insurance."

"You wouldn't have heard of us. We sell our operational risk management products directly to multi-nationals which are incorporated into salary packaging. But more importantly, I'm a fan of your mother's work. That's why I wanted you, you're a perfect fit."

It was only when Lilian had moved to Bondi that she had realised Dorothy was revered in Sydney.

Lilian felt a flicker of excitement. Finally, this meeting was starting to make sense.

48

William and Lilian sat on Tom's plush mint sofa. Their attempts at conversation had been thwarted by Dot's updates on Beth's game of Connect Four with their grandfather.

"Beth won. Now we're going to play Jenga," Dot yelled down from the front of the house then slammed the sliding door behind her, not waiting for her parents' reply.

Lilian cradled her tea, thinking about her week.

A grassy breeze wafted through an open window. It was cool outside. Melbourne couldn't decide whether it was winter or spring.

"What do I do that's fun?" Lilian asked.

"Is this another discussion about whether or not you're fun? You are, irrefutably, fun," William teased.

"A new client asked me what I do for fun," Lilian said with a contemplative frown.

"What did you say?" William found Lilian's introspections endearing, he'd replaced her journal as her sounding board.

"I didn't get a chance to reply because the meeting started."

"What were you going to say?"

Dot and Beth squealed in unison, Lilian and William paused expecting the door to fly open.

"I was going to make a joke about being too busy for fun because I just couldn't think of anything."

"Fun like a hobby?" William enquired, pondering what he did for fun.

"I guess." Lilian slipped into an analytic state and William watched her ruminate. "I don't do anything fun."

"I assume your new client wasn't intending to torment you with the question," William joked.

Lilian laughed. "She was not. Maddison's great. She's trying to poach me from Clarise." Lilian instantly regretted the comment. She didn't want to talk about work opportunities and hastily changed the subject. "You surf, that's fun."

Determined to be affirming, William lent over and kissed her tenderly. "I love you. You are perfect the way you are."

Lilian blushed, mindful of their family gathered in the other room. "Thank you."

The living room door flung open and Beth and Dot hurtled down the hall.

"Dad, swap, swaaaaap," Dot yelled.

Tom emerged, ready for a break.

"Jenga or Connect Four?" William conceded, parting from Lilian with a wink.

"Booooooth," Beth screeched as she ran back to the living room, Dot on her heels.

Spent, Tom sat opposite Lilian in his favourite armchair.

"I was going to let them win, but Dot actually beat me," he confessed, chuckling.

Lilian poured Tom strong tea from the pot.

"She's very good. Dot practices against Jordan."

Tom had met most of Lilian's family. "I'm glad you have siblings, or they'd have no cousins."

"Marcus and Tim are still galivanting overseas so who knows, there may be more out there," Lilian joked.

Tom had a distinct expression when he was thinking about Maggie, a fusion of joy and pain.

"We would have had more. We were older when we met. We tried."

Lilian was used to Tom's reminiscing. All roads led to Maggie.

"She would have updated this room by now. It was due for a change when," the phrase caught in Tom's throat, "she got sick."

Lilian had privately had the same thought. The seasonal fashion was baby green when Maggie died. Maggie hadn't warmed to the renovation. She preferred neutrals and would have been horrified to think her house would be green forever.

"Have you thought about redecorating?" Lilian asked, unsure whether the suggestion would be comforting or triggering.

Tom sucked in air as though the notion was harmful.

"I struggle with changing anything or getting rid of her things, but I know she would have hated it." He sighed wearily. "Maggie would have wanted me to sell the house and move on. I can't think of anything worse."

Lilian felt desperately sad. She was tempted to offer to help choose a new palette but the house felt sacred, like every mossy shade was a shrine to Maggie.

"She would be appalled at my wallowing," Tom remarked, ashamed by his grief.

"She would be doing the same thing," Lilian assured him. Tom and Maggie had barely spent a moment apart since they met.

Dot calmly exited the living room and walked down the hallway for some attention while William and Beth played Jenga.

Dot chose Maggie's armchair next to Tom which brought a tear to his eye.

"Are you okay, Grandpa?" Dot asked, getting up to hug him.

"I'm just very happy you're all here. These are happy tears." Tom picked Dot up and placed her gently on his knee. "We were talking about redecorating this room. What colour do you think it should be?"

Dot looked around the room, absorbing its greenness.

"White."

"Grandma would approve of your taste."

Lilian doubted Tom would ever tamper with Maggie's accidental legacy, but it was a relief he was thinking about the future.

"Beth beat me," William called, carrying Beth on his hip.

Tom and Lilian cheered.

William dropped Beth on the couch and she curled up next to Lilian, ready to fall asleep.

"Pizza then bed," William said to Beth then whispered to Lilian, "Once they're both asleep, we are going to do something fun."

49

Ari's harrowing sobs soaked through the wooden panels. Lilian stood with her hands pressed against the front door and tried to focus on her breathing. She was having a panic attack.

Knowing her life was about to change, Lilian lifted a quivering hand and knocked.

Lilian listened to heavy boots get louder as they approached.

Dale opened the door, dirty and gaunt. "Hi, Lil."

From the doorway Lilian could see Ari was on the floor, her limp body slumped over the coffee table.

Lilian forced her voice to rise. "Who?"

"Carlos," Dale confirmed coarsely and stood back for Lilian to pass him.

She muffled a shocked cry, tears flowed instantly. "Where are the kids?"

Ari, cocooned in her agony, hadn't noticed Lilian had arrived.

"At my house, with Kate. Ari hasn't told them yet," Dale said breathlessly.

Lilian had known the news was going to be grievous. She had been leaving the gym when she had received Ari's voice message. Ari's hideous pain was audible in her haunting words. *Come to the apartment. Now.*

Lilian broke out of her shock and went to her sister.

"Ari, I'm so sorry." Lilian wept and took Ari in her arms.

Ari nuzzled into Lilian and briefly stopped convulsing.

Lilian wanted to ask Dale what had happened to Carlos, but he had gone out to the balcony to compose himself.

Lilian and Ari sat on the living room floor in silence.

Ari resumed crying.

Ari's phone buzzed on the coffee table. Through her tears, Lilian relayed the message to Ari. "Mum says she is about to get on the plane so her phone will be off, but she should be here in a few hours."

Lilian assumed Dale must have called Dorothy.

Centred, Dale came back inside to update Lilian. "Kate will bring the kids home after Dorothy gets here. The police will be here soon. They need to ask Ari some questions."

Lilian's heart broke.

"Mum's going to tell Jordan. I can't do it." Ari spoke for the first time.

Lilian was angry Dale and Kate appeared to know more about what was going on with her family than she did.

"What happened?" Lilian demanded, frustrated, not wanting to be in the dark when the police arrived.

Ari deferred to Dale, unable to collate words to explain her nightmare.

"He was bitten by a snake while we were camping. The paramedics said he died in his sleep. They took him to the hospital for an autopsy," Dale relayed as heavy tears spilled onto his cheeks.

"He didn't feel the snake bite him?" Lilian exploded in disbelief.

"Apparently it bit his foot through the sleeping bag. They said the puncture wound wasn't very deep and they thought he probably wouldn't have felt the bite if his feet were cold," Dale explained between steadying breaths.

Ari retched at the imagery. She'd already thrown up everything in her stomach.

"Sorry," Dale whimpered.

Ari waved away his apology, she didn't blame him.

"Why were you camping somewhere with snakes?" Lilian snapped furiously.

"We weren't. There are never snakes at that campsite at this time of year, it's too cold."

Carlos and Dale had gone camping together every few months since they were teenagers. They were experienced hikers, they knew first aid, and they didn't take stupid risks.

Ari placed her hand on Lilian's arm, gesturing to spare Dale. Ari knew her loss was, simply, tragically, unlucky.

"Sorry, Dale. I'm just in shock," Lilian apologised. Dale looked exhausted. He'd just lost his best friend.

"I know, me too."

"Why are the police coming over?" Lilian asked.

"The paramedics called them. I convinced the officers to let me tell Ari about Carlos in person, but they said they still have to come to the apartment to do a formal notification." Dale shrugged, also uncertain why police were required.

Ari's grief switched from crying to trembling.

Lilian stroked her hair. "What do you need me to do?"

Ari tried, unsuccessfully, to sit up and focus.

"What do you need me to do," Ari repeated blankly, only able to think of her fatherless children.

Lilian's mind flashed back to their father's death. She recalled the moment the police had arrived at their house. Dorothy had collapsed. What happened next however was a childhood blur.

"Does his family know? The orchestra?" Lilian asked Dale.

"I called his sister. I haven't told the orchestra."

Lilian was about to ask about funeral plans when the bell rang. Dale left to open the door.

Lilian lifted Ari off the carpet and propped her against the arm of the couch.

"Can you get me some mouthwash?" Ari asked.

Lilian looked into her sister's eyes for the first time, and saw a sickening blackness had replaced her sparkle. Lilian didn't want to leave Ari's side, even to go to the bathroom.

"Of course," Lilian replied and kissed Ari's hair, then dashed to the ensuite.

Dale waited with the officers in the hall.

Lilian lifted the bottle to Ari's lips. She gagged at the contact then feebly dribbled the rinse into a cup.

"Ready?" Lilian asked.

She wasn't, but Ari nodded dutifully.

The sympathetic officers waited while Lilian wrapped her arms around Ari.

Lilian suddenly remembered William had back-to-back surgeries all day. Death didn't get him out of work. "I've got to pick Beth up from kindergarten. Will you be alright here with Dale while I find a sitter?"

"Go," Ari whispered, saving what was left of her energy to hear, again, how her husband had died.

Lilian closed the apartment door behind her and pulled out her phone to call William, but her tears were so thick she couldn't see the buttons.

50

Jane waved at Lilian from the entrance to Kirribilli Market.

Jane, in her high-end trench coat and exclusive designer handbag, was the epitome of sophistication. If Lilian hadn't witnessed Jane's transformation, she wouldn't have believed it.

"Thanks for coming." Lilian hugged Jane tightly.

"My goddaughters need me," Jane teased.

Dot had called Jane in France and asked her to come to Sydney and take care of Lilian because Lilian was really sad.

Determined not to disappoint Dot, who had never asked her for anything, Jane had put her meetings on hold and booked the next flight.

"I still don't know how she figured out how to call you," Lilian joked, chuffed Jane had dropped everything to be there for Carlos' funeral.

"It's nice to be wanted. I'm looking forward to seeing them." Jane smiled sorrily, wishing her visit had been compelled by happier circumstances.

They entered the market and were enveloped by a cloud of fragrances and fried foods.

"What are we buying?" Jane asked.

Lilian rummaged in her handbag for the shopping list.

"Wouldn't it be great if birthday parties stopped when

someone died." Lilian counted the names. "I need eight gifts."

"Wow," Jane replied, linking her arm with Lilian's. She scanned the stalls for toys. "I can't say I regret not having any."

Jane had married Pablo and moved to Paris soon after Dot was born. Her work in international law was renowned, her influence complemented her husband's powerful networks.

"Lucky for me, so you can take care of mine." Lilian's voice wobbled, grief was hitting her sporadically.

Jane rubbed her back. "Are you okay?"

Lilian considered a brave front, but realised she needed to vent. "I'm crying a lot."

Jane spotted a stack of recycled leather pencil cases and rummaged through the hodgepodge of pouches.

"We can double up on a couple of these presents. Half are for Dot's friends and half are for Beth's."

Jane selected two identical pink sleeves and handed cash to the maker. "Crying, anything else?"

Lilian and Jane were momentarily separated by a tour group charging through the crowd.

"I'm just tired and worried about Ari. Mum will be here for a few months to take care of the twins and Jordan while Ari runs the business, or vice versa. She isn't sure how she's going to feel."

"Dorothy's amazing. How are your girls coping?" Jane nudged Lilian toward a trestle covered with handmade crafts.

"Dot's upset, she's not sleeping. Beth doesn't really understand but she's unsettled by everyone else's moods." Lilian crossed out two names.

"What about William?" Jane rejected the stamps and stickers. "Too small, let's keep looking."

"He deals with death every day so it's not as confronting for him, but he's shocked."

"Were they close?" Jane asked. She wasn't privy to their daily lives.

"Not really. They didn't socialise outside the family." Lilian reflected on their spouses' awkward but affectionate friendship.

They approached the end of the market.

"Well, I'm glad I can be here for you and the girls this week," Jane said.

"I'm glad you're here too," Lilian echoed.

"Pablo's arriving tomorrow so I will have a shoulder to cry on," Jane noted, already missing her husband.

"Good, we're all going to need support."

Lacking inspiration, and clarity, Lilian stopped to re-consult the birthday list.

"I think bracelets or bows would be a safe bet," she said wearily.

"I saw some before." Jane u-turned to lead Lilian back to the jewellery stand and bumped into a tower of second-hand novels.

"Oh, I read your book on the plane," Jane remembered excitedly. "It was brilliant. I still can't believe you're friends with Rachel, but you two make a good team."

Lilian blushed. "Thank you, it was a lot of fun. Rachel wants us to write another."

"You should. Do you have time?" Jane wondered, assuming Lilian would be directing any spare attention to Ari.

"I can make time, but William might want to move back to Melbourne." Lilian forced the words to come out truthfully.

"Because of Tom?" Jane asked, surprised William would even consider the prospect.

"I'm oversimplifying, but essentially Tom is so heartsick his staff are worried he's going to make a mistake and inadvertently kill someone at work."

"I'm pretty sure there are regulators for that," Jane remarked cynically.

They reached the jewellery stand. Lilian had no recollection of passing it.

"These are perfect."

Jane began inspecting the tiny pieces, impressed by the quality.

"I started coming to the market because we would all turn up at parties with the same toy from the local store."

Jane saw through Lilian's deflection. "You don't want to go back to Melbourne?"

Lilian would have screamed 'No!' if they hadn't been surrounded by throngs of shoppers.

Jane could see the worry sitting behind the grief. "You think William would leave without you?"

Lilian was ashamed that she had contemplated the possibility. It felt like an unretractable betrayal to admit she had been lying in bed while her family slept, wondering whether William had the capacity to leave their children. The words escaped before she could stop them. "I think he might."

51

Lilian stared at her emails. The house was dark and quiet, and her thoughts were racing. She took a few deep breaths then went to brew a fresh pot of chamomile.

It had been an unusually taxing day. Lilian had spent the morning finalising funeral arrangements, then had met with Dot and Beth's teachers to update them on the situation at home. Afterward she had made a brief cameo at her office before rushing back to the school to collect Dot. Together they had sombrely shopped for funeral outfits before swinging back to the kindergarten for Beth.

Exhausted tears followed dinner, necessitating extensive cuddles before bed. William was working the same long distant hours he always had, but today it felt like Lilian was parenting alone.

Indulging a rare moment of self-pity, Lilian reminded herself to be grateful, then finally focused on answering Maddison's questions.

The home phone rudely disrupted her momentum.

"It's Al, sorry it's late," he quickly added, "Lily's fine."

Lilian appreciated the fast reassurance.

"Hi, Al. No problem. How are you?" She was picking Lily and Al up from the airport in the morning.

"I don't want you to worry, but we're not going to make it to the funeral. Lily's not feeling very well."

Lily had moved into Al's retirement village when Dorothy left to take care of Ari. Lily was too fall-prone to live alone.

"What's wrong?"

Al wanted to prepare Lilian gently, the timing would not be of their choosing. "Your grandmother is just old. She will only get weaker now."

Lilian noted the subtext.

"Al, if she's dying you need to tell us so we can say goodbye," Lilian snapped.

"She's not leaving us tomorrow, dear," Al replied kindly.

Vacating the terrace abruptly had unsettled Lily. Not knowing when she could go home had been agitating and grief bore heavily on her withering frame.

"Thanks for calling, Al. I'll let everyone know. Please give Lily our love," Lilian said apologetically.

"I will. Lily will call you in the morning." Al hung up.

Lilian's gratitude was fast replaced with despair. Her spiralling was diffused by the sound of William's keys in the front door.

Lilian was normally in bed when he arrived home from the hospital, and he was startled to find her working on the kitchen bench. His smile faded when he noticed the darkness under Lilian's eyes.

"Awful day?" William guessed and wrapped his arms around her.

"I'm tired," Lilian answered.

"How did it go at the school?" William asked, still at her side.

Lilian wanted to yell at him for having had to complete the days tasks alone, but Lilian knew she wasn't angry with him.

"Beth's teacher said she's been grumpy but doesn't seem to be too affected. Dot's teachers are worried about her. She's been having trouble concentrating and she's losing interest in her favourite subjects. Can you believe she didn't want to go to art class?"

William went to the fridge to find some food.

"I left you a plate in the oven."

"You're wonderful." William turned on the warmer and set about choosing a juice. "Sounds pretty normal for a kid dealing with grief."

Lilian didn't want to impart the rest of the conversation, but she didn't have the right to omit information when it came to their daughters.

"Apparently the school has been worried about her for a while." Lilian held back tears, humiliated she'd been educated on the wellbeing of her own daughter. "They had been planning to invite us in for a meeting before Carlos died."

"Why?" William asked.

Lilian and William rarely discussed parenting, they were generally in sync.

"Dot told her teacher we are going to break up. Apparently Dot said you're never home and you go away a lot." Lilian sighed. The truth was unsweetenable.

"But we have always explained everything to her? She knows my job is demanding and Dad needs me."

"I know. I haven't asked her about it yet. I wanted to tell you first. Maybe at that age the reason doesn't matter." Lilian's heart broke at William's expression.

"I'm sorry," William pleaded for forgiveness.

"You don't have to apologise to me. We made those decisions together," Lilian reassured him.

"I have to talk to her," William declared, determined to fix the situation.

Lilian paused, deliberating how to phrase what needed to be said.

"And say what? You aren't going to change." Lilian tried to sound supportive, but it was too harsh.

"That was fast. I thought we were in this together?"

He pulled his hand away from her knee and went to check the oven.

"I am in this with you, but Dot feels the way she feels because you choose to be elsewhere, rather than here with her. I don't resent your choices, but she's a child. She doesn't care why you're not here."

Lilian regretted that he was hurt but William needed to hear it. An apology to Dot was only going to be patronising, or worse, condescending.

"You just said she's worried I'm going to leave, not that she's upset because I'm away."

Lilian stared at him. She was too tired to debate semantics. She didn't want the next sentence to leave her mouth. It was irreversible, so she waited for him to speak.

William placed his hands on the counter in frustration. Realising too late he'd forced the point they'd both been avoiding.

52

Lilian and William had been positioned in the second pew. They huddled together. William with one arm around Lilian and one arm around Dot, Beth on Lilian's lap.

It had been a morning from hell. Upon learning Lily wasn't coming for the funeral, Dot had become distressed and decided she wasn't going. Beth, confused by the strength of her sister's aversion, clung to Dot and refused to let go. Jane offered to take the girls to the library instead. After William and Lilian had reluctantly left for the service Dot had realised that if she didn't go Jordan would be alone. Dot then became hysterical and demanded Jane take them to the church.

Lilian sat behind Ari who clutched Jordan. To Ari's other side, Connie and Abbie sat flanked by Dorothy. The twins, too young to comprehend the occasion, played happily, unaffected by the grown-ups around them. Every now and then Ari would touch the twins or Dorothy, or reach around and hold Lilian's hand, checking on her family amidst her suffering.

The eulogies were long and, despite Carlos' exuberance, the service was miserable. His family were inconsolable and could barely speak. His colleagues and friends tried to celebrate his life, but the well-meaning anecdotes were tainted with the injustice everyone felt.

Dale spoke heartfully about his devout friend. He was visibly traumatised, but determined for Jordan to honour Carlos' memory.

Ari was last to speak. She let go of Jordan and summoned her strength, but she couldn't stand.

William lifted Beth onto his lap and Lilian went to assist Ari.

"You can do this," Lilian whispered as she wedged her forearm under her sister's armpit then hoisted Ari onto her feet.

Once up, Ari steadied then stepped slowly toward the podium.

Lilian returned to her seat. Shattered for her sister, she leant into William who held her tightly.

"Thank you all for coming," Ari began groggily, like she wasn't sure whether she was awake. "I know none of us want to be here."

Ari's words trailed off. Gathering her thoughts, she inhaled deeply and started again.

"I was in love with my husband from the moment I met him. It was always hard for me to reconcile that we were so happy when our whole relationship was a series of accidents."

There were a few half-hearted laughs.

"Most of you know our stories. We met because I left my phone on a train and Carlos found it and tracked me down. I got pregnant with Jordan because I took aspirin instead of the pill. An obsessed fan left Carlos our apartment. Whenever I would point out that our happiness was so precarious, Carlos would say it was fate. Only my gentle kind husband could look at all this chaos and coincidence and conclude our beautiful messy mistakes were fate."

Ari paused to wipe away her tears.

"I know everyone here is devastated. I am devastated. But I know what Carlos would say if he was here. He would say it was fate. He lived his life with no regrets. He died doing something he loved, with someone he loved. He wasn't in pain." Ari swallowed a sob. "He knew his family were safe. Carlos wouldn't have wanted to go any other way."

The peace Ari conveyed was the reassurance her husband's loved ones needed at the end of an otherwise tragic service. Lilian was moved by Ari's gracious words for Carlos' family.

The formalities concluded and William took Dot and Beth home for a nap.

Lilian stayed with Ari who stood at the exit, accepting condolences, as family and friends left to go back to her apartment to continuing mourning together.

When the chamber was finally empty, Ari collapsed onto a pew.

"I'm relieved that's over." She sighed loudly.

"You were wonderful." Lilian was immensely proud.

"I don't quite believe it yet, but I'll get there," Ari replied.

Lilian wasn't sure whether Ari meant she didn't believe her husband dying was fate, or that he had died at all. "Is there anything I can do?"

"Probably." Ari smiled against the tears. "I'm on autopilot."

Lilian was impressed her sister could muster humour.

Ari stared at the casket, consumed by her thoughts.

"Do you want some time alone to say goodbye?" Lilian offered.

"No, I'm not saying goodbye." Ari exhaled painfully.

She gripped Lilian's hand, waiting for the burst of agony to mellow.

Dorothy joined them and took hold of Ari's other hand. "Dale and Kate are taking Jordan and the twins with them to the apartment."

"Thanks, Mum," Ari said, grateful for Dorothy's support.

"We should head back soon," Dorothy prompted, aware from experience walking away was the hardest part.

They sat for a long time, each pondering what lay ahead. Lilian was comforted by her mother's presence and the knowledge that they'd been through this before.

Ari stood and approached the casket. She lay her cheek on the pine. Her sobs were gut-wrenching. Lilian and Dorothy sat arm in arm and watched her cry. She kissed the lid, leaving a bright red lip mark, then whispered her farewell.

53

Jane raised her champagne glass. "Here's to Rachel and Charlie."

Lilian and Rachel clinked their flutes together.

"And here's to Rachel allowing me to crash your engagement drinks on my last night in town," Jane added.

"It's my pleasure. Actually I crashed your last night in town with my engagement," Rachel gushed.

Lilian was relieved Jane and Rachel were getting along, and slightly concerned by how well.

"Who proposed?" Jane asked.

Lilian had barely spoken to Rachel since Carlos died and was thankful to receive some good news.

"What's a romantic way to say she-wore-me-down-over-time?" Rachel laughed.

"Don't be rude," Lilian chided, although the depiction was fairly accurate.

"No more questions from me," Jane joked.

"Sorry, that sounded terrible. Charlie has wanted to get engaged for years. Marriage doesn't mean anything to me, so it always felt disingenuous to say yes. In the end, I'm happy to wear more jewellery and sign a contract if it makes her feel safe."

"That's sweet," Jane cooed.

"What about yourself?" Rachel asked, pointing to Jane's

bespoke wedding ring.

"Pablo wanted me to move to France. I said I wouldn't go unless we were married. I wasn't sure he was serious, and I wasn't going to leave my UN post without a commitment. I wish my story was more romantic than an ultimatum."

"There was a sensational proposal, after Pablo agreed to the ultimatum," Lilian joked.

"That's true, forced romance," Jane concurred, sipping champagne.

Lilian didn't need to share her story. Jane and Rachel both knew William had turned up in Canberra with a ring handed down from Maggie's mother and asked Lilian to move to Sydney with him.

"Trouble in paradise?" Rachel guessed in response to Lilian's worried expression.

"Not sure," Lilian admitted. "William wants us to move back to Melbourne so he can take over from Tom."

"What do you want?" Jane asked.

"Our lives are here and my family is here. I don't see a future in Melbourne when everyone I love is in Sydney."

"Dorothy and Lily are in Melbourne," Rachel noted.

"Dorothy is planning on moving back after Lily dies which accordingly to Al will be soon. And Marcus and Tim will end up back in Sydney eventually."

The waiter arrived to hand out the tapas menu.

"One of everything please. My treat," Jane said, and the waiter left with their order.

"Does William want to move back permanently?" Rachel asked, her next sip emptying the glass.

Jane reached across the small bar table to top up Rachel's flute, but they had run out of champagne.

"I don't know, we're both avoiding the conversation."

Lilian recalled the late night stand off in the kitchen, which ended with her leaving William to eat dinner alone.

"I'm going to say something indelicate," Jane warned.

Lilian laughed, appreciative of the notice. "Please do."

Rachel lent forward intently and placed her elbows on the table.

"You both knew your families lived in different cities when you got married. Have you not talked about this before?"

The comment from anyone else would have been insulting. Jane however was genuinely curious.

"I agreed to move to Sydney because that's where William was going for his surgery promotion when we got engaged. The decision had nothing to do with my family or his. We've never had a conversation about where we wanted to live in the future. We've only ever moved for our jobs."

"Interesting," Jane said.

Lilian wondered whether William's answer would mirror hers.

"But regardless it's not about us anymore. Dot and Jordan are best friends, and Beth hates change. It's about what's best for our kids and they would want to stay here." Lilian felt defensive on behalf of her girls. "Sorry, Rachel, I've taken over your celebration."

"Not at all," Rachel said, dismissing the apology. "All good learning points for a newly engaged woman. When I get home, I'm going to get it in writing that Charlie will never try and make me leave Sydney."

The first of the tapas arrived and Jane ordered more champagne and a cocktail list.

Rachel and Jane were avoiding eye contact.

"Thank you both for listening. I haven't had much time to think lately," Lilian said self-consciously.

Jane kindly changed the topic.

"Guess what I got in the mail last month?" She paused for dramatic effect. "An invitation from the law school to our ten-year reunion!"

Lilian had already declined. She was provisionally avoiding all conversations about going to Melbourne.

"That's exciting. I had my undergrad reunion last year," Rachel replied.

Lilian noticed Rachel's sudden change in temperament.

"I doubt I'll be able to get back for it, but I would have loved to have seen everyone again," Jane said regretfully.

"Even Luke?" Lilian teased.

Jane laughed, blushing at the memory of her disparate first love. "I forgot about him. Yes, even that little cheater."

"Was he in a band?" Rachel thought she vaguely remembered a Luke from a student club.

"He was in a band. He moved to America to tour, no idea what happened to him after that. Maybe he was wildly successful," Jane speculated. "Speaking of exes, did you keep in touch with Jamie?"

Rachel turned the colour of the maraschino cherry atop her champagne glass.

"He's not my ex, but I did run into him at a party recently," she confirmed awkwardly, stuffing an arancini ball into her mouth to discourage further questioning.

"Really." Jane gasped theatrically. "How is Jamie?"

Lilian was surprised Rachel hadn't mentioned the rendezvous before now.

Rachel swallowed then sped through her confession. "He was good. Still gorgeous, married with kids, partner at his firm, asked about Lilian."

"Asked about Lilian," Jane repeated.

"He'd heard we wrote a book together," Rachel said guiltily to Lilian. "I told him you were married, with kids, and not available."

"Why are you acting like you did something wrong?" Lilian queried, perplexed.

"He asked me to give you his phone number. He wanted to meet you for a coffee." Rachel plunged her jealous face into cupped hands, mortified she'd been so spiteful.

Lilian laughed at Rachel's lingering crush, amazed her dear friend had deliberately withheld the message. "I don't care, I don't want to see Jamie. I'm married."

Jane burst out laughing. "For now."

54

"Welcome," Maddison sang as Lilian stepped out of the elevator. She held an access pass in one hand and a bouquet in the other.

"Good morning." Lilian quickly buttoned up her suit jacket and checked for signs of parenting.

"You look great," Maddison reassured her as she thrust the flowers at Lilian then lassoed the lanyard over her neck.

Lilian forced a smile. "Thanks."

"Desk or introductions first?" Maddison asked.

Dion hung back, organising documents in a folder, waiting for Maddison's direction.

"Desk please," Lilian chose, keen to rid herself of the overbearing gift.

"Great choice. Dion, please let Alloysius and Nabine know we will be by shortly," Maddison said, leading Lilian toward a security door.

Dion curtsied then skipped away to complete the task.

"You will need your pass to get into the building. You can go anywhere anytime, you have full access. Have a try."

Lilian swiped her pass against the panel and the door popped open.

"Alloysius is the head of legal and Nabine is the head of accounting," Maddison explained as she led the way.

The tenancy spanned the breadth of the floor. Offices lined the glazed perimeter with generous open plan cubicles in the centre. The space was mostly empty, a handful of people milled about quietly.

"Most of our staff work from home. When everyone is here, the office gets quite rowdy." Maddison winked. "Toilets and the kitchenette are down that corridor to the left and this is your office."

Lilian noted the floor plan and tried to orient herself to the amenities.

"Where's your office?"

"Good question. At the end of this row." Maddison pointed. "Alloysius is in the opposite corner to me and Nabine is opposite you, on the other side of the cubicles."

Maddison turned back to Lilian's office door and gestured to the security panel.

Lilian swiped in. The dark mahogany desk and regal furniture reminded her of Professor Matthews.

"I apologise if it's too formal. We can make it friendlier if you'd like?"

"It's gorgeous. Honestly, I love it," Lilian insisted.

Lilian wasn't expecting to be allocated her own space. Maddison seemed to read her mind.

"You need an office because you will be having confidential conversations about our finances. Lots of sticky ears out there in the middle."

"Understood," Lilian replied, appreciative of the privacy.

Dion appeared and brazenly tapped his watch.

"I'll take you to meet the team and don't forget to keep your pass on." Maddison darted out the door, recommencing the tour.

Lilian placed her briefcase on the couch and looked around

for somewhere to put the flowers.

"Dion will bring a vase," Maddison yelled from halfway down the hall.

Lilian rested the base of the bunch in the wastepaper bin then followed Maddison out the door. She caught up as they arrived at a meeting room.

"Alloysius will take over from here," Maddison said.

Alloysius and Nabine were waiting with broad smiles and laptops open.

"Have a good meeting. When you're done here, Dion will show you the emergency exits." Maddison reversed then sped away.

"Thank you, Maddison," Lilian called.

Alloysius stood and vigorously shook Lilian's hand. "Welcome, Lilian. I'm Alloysius and this is Nabine."

"We're so excited to meet you," Nabine added eagerly.

"I'm happy to be here." Lilian sat next to Nabine and opened her laptop.

Alloysius and Nabine shared a tense glace.

Lilian waited for Alloysius to continue the introduction.

"We are so grateful you agreed to work with us," Nabine said cautiously.

Lilian wondered why Nabine appeared so nervous.

"How can I help?" Lilian prompted, certain the meeting was headed somewhere she wasn't expecting.

"We're in a bit of a pickle at the minute," Alloysius said.

Nabine frowned at Alloysius.

"We are in a lot of a pickle," Nabine corrected.

"How so?" Lilian asked calmly. She was used to clients under and overstating the truth. She reserved her angst for the numbers.

"In our defence, Lilian, the company grew far quicker than we were expecting. Maddison is a wonderful salesperson," Alloysius said, mounting his lawyerly defence.

Lilian intervened impartially. "No one's on trial. I'm here because you need a tax lawyer. Just start from the start."

Nabine sighed, grateful for Lilian's confidence.

"We're in trouble with the Tax Commissioner," Alloysius admitted, comforted by Lilian's temperament.

"What kind of trouble?"

Dion waved through the window as he raced to deliver the vase to Lilian's office.

"The Commissioner wrote to Maddison and told her we don't understand how to complete a Business Activity Statement, or how to calculate Goods and Services Tax, and she needs to get a tax lawyer," Nabine blurted.

Lilian masterfully hid her amusement at the blistering rebuke.

Alloysius nodded with reluctant confirmation. "I'm a contract lawyer. I don't know what's in the tax rulings. I can't even find them on the Tax Office website."

"Don't sell yourselves short. You helped Maddison build this company from scratch. That's an amazing achievement," Lilian said, trying to salvage what was left of their self-esteem.

"Thank you, Lilian. It's great to have you on board." Alloysius blushed, inspired by Lilian's positivity.

Nabine beamed.

It seemed rectifying Maddison's non-compliance was going to be immense, just when her family needed her full attention. But Lilian was heartened by their humility, and surprised to be energised by the challenge. "Likewise, Alloysius. Let's get to work."

55

Ari and Lilian watched on in hysterics as Jordan upstaged Dot and her friends at the barre. The posse huffed and sooked, ruffled by the imposter's superior agility.

"Well, this is unexpected." Ari clapped, delighted.

So far, Ari had held herself together throughout Dot's birthday party. Lilian knew Ari would crash soon. Joy was now chased with misery when Ari remembered she was unable to share the experience with Carlos.

"I still can't believe he came." Lilian laughed.

Dot had begged Jordan to join her ballet class party. After soulful contemplation Jordan's adoration of Dot had prevailed and he had asked Ari to buy him a leotard.

"He really is a natural," Lilian marvelled, as Jordan glided through the air.

"Just when I thought this week couldn't get any funnier," Ari replied, equally impressed.

Ari was referring to Dorothy's lover turning up at her apartment and demanding to know why Dorothy had broken up with him.

"How is Juan?" Lilian wondered.

"I suspect he's been hospitalised with shock."

"It's a lot to take in," Lilian agreed sympathetically.

Ari had described Juan in her voicemails as the youngest, hottest man she'd ever seen.

"I don't know who was more startled, me or him." Ari was close to dual purpose tears. "I should have taken a photo."

"Where did she meet him?" Lilian asked, curious.

"I have no idea. I know nothing about him. They left together and Mum came back half an hour later and wouldn't tell me anything." Ari shook her head in feigned disapproval.

"How did he know where you live?" Lilian frowned, hoping the grand gesture was a welcome surprise.

"Apparently a mutual friend gave him my address. They assumed he knew we existed, normal people don't pretend they don't have adult children."

The ballet instructor was so enthralled with Jordan she'd left the group with her assistant to teach him a solo. Thankfully, Dot appeared to be pleased her cousin was excelling.

"I hope he's alright," Lilian commented.

"Juan or Jordan?" Ari was too slow to stifle a burst of laughter, drawing scowls from the girls trying to concentrate.

"Both," Lilian joked.

"Juan seemed shattered. I'm not sure what Mum did to him," Ari said as seriously as she could manage while she caught her breath.

"I hope they work it out. He seems to genuinely care for her," Lilian said.

"He's seriously at least ten years younger than her, maybe more."

"So what? If he doesn't want kids, what does it matter."

"No judgement." Ari threw her hands up playfully.

The instructor was wrapping up. Lilian checked her phone.

"No William?" Ari said, noticing Lilian's pensive glance.

"He's probably stuck in theatre." Lilian glared at her empty inbox, willing William to call.

"He would be here if he could."

Lilian masked a flash of irritation. William could have been at the party if he'd taken the day off work. But these days, he saved all his leave to fly to Melbourne. Lilian didn't want to complain about her disappointing husband to her widowed sister.

"Will Dot be upset?" Ari asked.

William had explained to Dot that he might not be out of surgery in time for her party. It was heartbreaking to watch her daughter realise she was so far down her father's list of priorities that she couldn't even rely on him on her birthday. Lilian felt furious on Dot's behalf. Dot, fortunately, had shrugged it off.

"I think she's developed low expectations," Lilian admitted bitterly.

"Having a surgeon for a father can't be easy," Ari empathised.

Lilian could feel herself getting upset and took a slow breath. She didn't want Dot to be distracted by her emotions, her eldest was highly perceptive.

The instructor opened the door to the gallery and the ballerinas tumbled out and into the arms of their chaperones.

Pointes were unstrung and replaced with strappy sandals while the families coordinated with Lilian to meet at a café for afternoon tea.

Ari pulled Lilian aside.

"Jordan's wrecked. I'm going to take him home and, I don't know, do a cool down or maybe an ice bath? Thanks for today, it was nice to laugh."

She twinged at the admission of enjoyment.

"Anytime. Call William if you need some advice," Lilian added, appreciating the irony of the suggestion.

"I will." Ari collected Jordan from his goodbye with Dot.

Parents began to herd children out of the studio and load them into back seats.

Dot hurried Lilian to the car, not wanting to be late for her own birthday cake.

Clarise came over, Min hobbling beside her.

"Hey, we're going to head off. Min's got a nasty blister," Clarise apologised.

Min nestled at her mother's side, propped on one leg.

"No problem," Lilian assured them. "Min, are you all right?"

Min nodded tiredly.

"I'll give your lolly bag to Mum at work."

Min nodded, her knee starting to quiver.

"It will be nice to see you at the office, everyone's missing you," Clarise commented.

"I'm missing them too. I've just been so busy with Ari, and Maddison, and the kids."

"I don't think Maddison's going to let you go," Clarise joked nervously.

Lilian appeased her worried friend. "Maddison won't have a choice. See you next week, I promise."

Hearing herself list excuses, Lilian realised she hadn't missed her job at Bondi Singh at all.

56

Lilian clutched the golf buggy as it meandered through the lush grounds.

"It's enormous," she remarked as the usher pulled up to Al's villa. Lilian collected her overnight bag from the front seat.

"We get that a lot," the usher replied, then sped off, leaving Lilian to try and find the entrance.

The front door was obscured from the path by a bulky banana palm. Lilian rang the bell and waited.

"Lilian." Al opened the door and pulled her in for a hug.

"Hi, Al." Lilian returned the squeeze.

Al unwrapped his cardigan clad arms.

Lilian stepped into the foyer and took in the bright and cosy room. "The estate is stunning."

"It is rather charming," Al whispered as though he was in trouble. "She's in the sunroom."

He led the way, pausing at each painting hanging in the hall for Lilian to admire his artworks.

"I didn't realise you're a collector?"

"I'm not. Just a long life, plenty of time to distil." Al chuckled and shuffled along.

They arrived at the sunroom.

"Enter at your own peril," Al joked quietly.

Lilian smiled. Al was adorable. She was grateful he'd called last night.

"Lilian's here to see you, I'll make some tea," Al called loudly enough for Lily to hear, then plodded off to the kitchen.

Lily didn't respond, so Lilian pushed open the door.

Lily was sitting in a wicker chair with a cup of tea staring out the window at a mini-lake awash with water flowers sited in the middle of a ring of villas.

"I'm not talking to him," Lily snapped.

"Okay," Lilian said, trying not to appear dismissive of her grandmother's seemingly unjustified grudge.

"I don't want to be married to a dobber. He had no right to call you."

A frog bounced across the lawn.

Devoid of a strategy to defuse Lily's mood, Lilian didn't respond.

"Well, you're here now. What do you want?" Lily turned and glared at Lilian.

"I want to convince you not to cancel your party," Lilian replied, mindful not to appear Al-sided.

"I don't want to live here. I miss my terrace. I want to go home," Lily yelled and slammed her fist on a cushion.

"Whoa. Can you not break your own arm please," Lilian said, disturbed by the aggressive outburst and placed her bag down on the checkerboard tiles to hug Lily.

Lily reluctantly hugged back.

Lilian let go and sat opposite Lily on the padded bench which ran under the windowsill. It was a beautiful room with a spectacular view. The bitsy courtyard at the terrace paled in comparison.

Lily's fury subsided, slightly. "It is lovely to see you."

"I don't know what's going on with you and Al, but we would have found out the party had been cancelled when everyone turned up at the Marina and you weren't there."

"Don't take his side," Lily demanded.

"I'm not taking anyone's side, but I'm glad Al called because you didn't. The family are looking forward to celebrating with you," Lilian pleaded diplomatically.

Lily crossed her arms, irritated at having to justify herself.

"I don't feel like celebrating and the party is just a hassle for everyone."

"No one thinks that. Why do you think that?" Lilian asked, alarmed by Lily's baseless claim.

"All my grandchildren and my great-grandchildren and even my own daughter have to waste an entire weekend to get here and I don't want the fuss. Especially when everyone is grieving."

Lilian's heart sank. The trip wasn't a hassle at all.

"Lily, I don't know where this is coming from. Everyone is excited about the trip."

Al knocked on the door then entered, not waiting to be denied entry.

"I'm just dropping off the tea, then I'm heading over to the club," he announced before Lily could scold him for interrupting.

"Thanks, Al," Lilian said, and he gave her a wink as he closed the door.

Lily had twisted away from Al to ensure there was no doubt she was ignoring him.

"I want to go home," Lily spat, reminded she was supposed to be angry.

Lilian poured boiling water from a dainty pot into a matching cup and saucer and chose a tea bag from the selection Al had fanned on the tray.

"This is very thoughtful," Lilian noted supportively, certain Al had done nothing to warrant Lily's wrath.

Lily ignored the comment.

Lilian returned to the heart of the problem. "Mum will probably be in Sydney with Ari for a while. Would you like me to find you a homecare nurse so you can move back into the terrace?"

"Yes. I want a nurse. I want to go home," Lily agreed instantly, smiling for the first time since Lilian had arrived.

"Can you stay here with Al a bit longer? It might take me some time to find someone you like."

Lily contemplated the query, reflecting on her unfair behaviour.

"Al has been wonderful. I'm just grieving." Lily paused. "I'm so angry. I've lost a husband, a son, and now a grandson. It's too much."

Lilian had suspected this episode wasn't about the party, or Al. But Lily was nonetheless right, Al was practically an informant for her family in Sydney.

"I'm sorry you've been here alone, while we've been grieving together. I should have visited sooner," Lilian apologised, feeling ashamed she'd not realised Lily needed them. Lilian had become too reliant on Al's insights.

"Darling, no, you have little ones," Lily said, dismissing Lilian's guilt.

"Little ones who are going to be crushed their great-grandmother isn't having a fabulous party," Lilian cajoled.

"Well in that case, I wouldn't want them to be disappointed," Lily conceded.

Mission accomplished, Lilian thought, relieved she'd made the effort.

57

William had taken Lilian to an Italian restaurant recommended by a patient. The main meal had been delicious, then William had uncharacteristically ordered dessert.

They'd spent the start of their date syncing calendars, scheduling, and ensuring there were no childcare gaps. William hadn't taken his hand off Lilian's thigh all night. It made Lilian nervous when he was clingy. The gesture was, historically, a precursor to a difficult conversation.

"Are you alright?" Lilian asked, after the barista had left with their coffee order.

William took back his hand and shifted to the other side of the booth.

"Doug and I spoke to Dad last week. We told him about Shirley's intervention," William began. "I'm sorry I didn't get a chance to tell you before now."

Lilian wasn't upset. They never bothered to try to have adult conversations in the house. Without fail they would be interrupted by a screaming match, or a cut knee, and then they would both be anxious until they could resume the discussion.

"How did Tom take it?" Lilian asked.

"Dad was mortified. He said he wasn't feeling his best but didn't think his mood was affecting his work."

"I'm glad Doug was there to back you up," Lilian said, pleased William had progressed the issue.

"Doug was great, he told Dad he needed to take leave while he sorted himself out," William added.

Lilian was grateful Doug had had the courage to do what William wouldn't.

"What's Tom going to do at home all day? Wasn't that what everyone was trying to avoid, Tom being miserable and alone?"

"Dad's planning on publishing some research articles and redecorating the house."

After months of worry, Lilian doubted the solution was so simple.

"He seems good so far. He's been going down to the Marina for lunch with Doug most days this week."

"In that case, how much longer will you be going to Melbourne now that Tom can come and stay with us in Sydney?"

William winced.

Lilian braced for impact.

"I've been thinking. And… I still want to go back and live in Melbourne, us and the kids."

Lilian could hear her heart beating in her ears.

A waiter interrupted to deliver a giant serving of tiramisu and two spoons.

"After Mum died, I felt obliged to go back to take care of Dad. I spoke to Doug, and I realised I want to go back and run the Clinic," William explained the context to add weight to his outlandish proposition.

Lilian was shocked. It wasn't the conversation she thought she was going to have tonight. "You want to leave surgery?"

"No, but I never see you. I never see the kids. I love surgery but I can't get missed birthday parties back. There are no second chances."

Lilian wanted to be angry, but it was clear William was angry enough at himself.

"I want to experience running our family business with Dad, even just for a few years. It's a memory I want to have when he's gone, and not because he's a hazard." William attempted a charming smile.

The tiramisu was still untouched when their coffees arrived.

Lilian took a sip of her latte and a mouthful of sponge, to buy time before she had to reply.

"Anything else?" she asked, suspending her reaction until she had all the facts.

"Not that I can think of at the moment," William confirmed, lifting a heaped spoon to his mouth.

William's fantasy sounded to Lilian like a decision dressed up as a discussion.

"Just to clarify, you want to leave surgery to spend more time with me and the girls?"

"Yes," William replied, momentarily distracted by the decadent cream.

"What I mean is, if we don't want to go to Melbourne, are you still going to leave your job and be a nine-to-five doctor so you can spend more time with us in Sydney?"

William considered the proposition.

"I would love the girls to have the same experience I had growing up at the Clinic. I loved it, they're my family," William replied, not addressing Lilian's question.

Lilian felt herself getting irritated.

"William, you're asking me to uproot our family so our children can relive your childhood when they are perfectly happy where they are."

William was taken aback by Lilian's rebuttal.

"We're just having a conversation. I'm telling you what I've been thinking about lately. Are we not doing that anymore? Talking about our future?" William sulked defensively and crossed his arms.

"Doesn't sound like a conversation. It sounds like you've decided we're moving to Melbourne," Lilian increased her volume, determined for him to hear her. "I'm not moving."

"So you're not even going to think about it?" William said, astonished by Lilian's rejection.

"No, I don't need to think about it, because I don't want to go."

They stared at each other. Lilian holding her ground on behalf of her girls who had been through enough this year.

William broke the stare and started poking the neglected dessert.

"If you want to quit surgery so you can spend more time with our daughters, I'm fully supportive of that. But we aren't going anywhere." Lilian hovered over her next words, mindful they couldn't be taken back. "If you want to go to Melbourne, you're going alone."

58

"Thanks for coming." Dorothy closed Ari's front door behind Lilian.

"Of course. Where is she?" Lilian hung her soaked raincoat on a clothes peg.

"Bathroom floor," Dorothy answered.

"How long has she been in there?" Lilian peeled off her soaked boots and socks.

"About three hours." Dorothy handed Lilian a towel. "There's a fresh pot of coffee on the bench."

"Thanks. What happened?" Lilian sponged water from her hair.

"Nothing specific, just the usual." Dorothy took a dry umbrella from the closet.

Juan had convinced Dorothy to meet him for lunch to discuss a reconciliation.

"Okay, have fun," Lilian replied, cheekily, ready to take over.

Lilian left Dorothy armouring to battle the weather and went to check on Ari.

She knocked on the closed door.

"I'm coming in," Lilian called softly then opened the door to find Ari face down on the tiles, still in pyjamas. "You look uncomfortable. Do you want to move to the couch?"

"I like the tiles. They're cold," Ari said from under the blanket Dorothy had laid over most of her. "I like the sound of the rain."

Ari wasn't like this every day. Some days were better than others.

"Alright." Lilian tried not to laugh and retrieved a couch cushion for herself and joined Ari on the floor. "Did something happen this morning?"

Ari shuddered from the cold and rolled over on to her back to face Lilian. Her eye sockets were black, and she looked exhausted.

"The girls are forgetting him," Ari said, her voice heavy with sorrow.

Lilian wasn't sure what to say.

"They remember him sometimes, like bedtime, or bathtime, but generally they're happy, like nothing changed."

Lilian doubted it was that simple. The twins were affected, but what Lilian thought was irrelevant.

"I'm going to miss Carlos forever, and Jordan will miss him, and his sisters won't know why we're sad because they won't remember him." Ari exhaled slowly, closing her eyes.

Lilian didn't comment that she and Ari had been in the same situation with Marcus and Tim when they were growing up.

"Is lying on the floor making you feel better?" Lilian asked, not grasping the correlation between the floor and solace.

Ari laughed. "Is this tough love?"

"Sorry, no, I just don't get it?"

Ari smiled. Typical Lilian.

"If I stay here with my eyes closed, I can't see anything that reminds me I have to keep living without my husband," Ari explained. "I can pretend my daughters care their dad died."

"That's not fair. They're two years old. Abbie and Connie were obsessed with Carlos. You know they care," Lilian said, defending her nieces who weren't old enough to speak for themselves.

Ari pulled herself up onto her elbows and noticed her sister slumped awkwardly against the bathroom wall.

"Where are you supposed to be?" Ari asked, aware her grief was inconveniencing everyone around her.

"I cancelled a meeting with a client. Mum will be back in an hour then I've got to pick Beth up from kindergarten." Lilian's patience was beginning to thin. "Where are you supposed to be?"

"I was going to work from home," Ari replied. "The twins are at daycare and Jordan's at school. Mum will pick them up later."

Lilian pondered whether it was uncouth to call Ari out on her exploitative wallowing. "Can't you pick up your kids?"

Ari frowned. "That's harsh."

"No, it isn't. Mum can't put her life on hold forever," Lilian refuted flatly.

"Her life taking care of Lily," Ari said rudely.

"Exactly, Mum spends all her time taking care of other people. If you can't run her business and take care of your kids, then find someone to replace you," Lilian replied, not sure how they ended up having this conversation.

Ari shot up, swaying as she adjusted to being vertical. "Did you come over to criticise me when I'm down? Literally!"

"No, I came over so Mum could go on a date because you were flat on the floor with no awareness that she needed to be somewhere else." Lilian felt herself getting annoyed.

Ari was too stunned by her sister's tone to consider Lilian's sentiment may carry some merit.

"I can't believe you're accusing me of being selfish while I'm grieving my dead husband," Ari yelled and stormed out of the bathroom.

Lilian picked the bedding off the floor and followed Ari into the kitchen.

"I'm not trying to insult you. This," Lilian pointed at the bathroom, "is not just about Carlos. You were relying on Mum before Carlos died."

Ari was fuming. She filled up the kettle, slammed it down on the stove, then stomped back to the bathroom and kicked the door shut.

"Don't bother telling me to go, I'm not going anywhere," Lilian called from the kitchen.

She sat on the couch and waited for Ari to return.

When the kettle had boiled, Lilian brewed calming ginger tea and then knocked on the bathroom door. "Your tea's ready when you are."

Ari opened the door, took the mug, then slammed the door in Lilian's face.

Lilian sat on the couch and scrolled through her emails on her phone, waiting for Ari to come out.

She cracked the door open a smidge. Ari had fallen asleep, so Lilian carefully placed the blanket back over her intransigent sister.

When Dorothy arrived back at the apartment, Ari was still hibernating.

"How is she?" Dorothy asked, beaming from her date.

"Napping and angry at me. How was Juan?"

"Good." Dorothy blushed. "What happened?

Lilian smiled triumphantly. "I told her to pick up her own kids."

59

Lilian listened to Nabine's team celebrating in the cubicles. They'd submitted the Business Activity Statement and, for the first time, did not fear a dressing-down from the Commissioner.

Nabine peered around the door frame. Lilian was still working.

"Please, Lilian, join us. You have done so much, the team want to thank you," Nabine beckoned in her warm soft tone.

It had been gratifying seeing Nabine come alive as her confidence grew under Lilian's tutelage.

"Thanks, Nabine. I will give this month a miss, I'm just finishing up."

"Next month then?" Nabine asked, disappointed.

"Absolutely," Lilian promised.

Nabine reluctantly accepted the postponement and went back to her charges.

Lilian packed up for the night. She didn't need to take the laptop, she'd be back tomorrow.

Maddison wanted to see her but Lilian needed to get home. William was taking Jordan to the basketball.

Maddison was on the phone. She motioned to Lilian to come in.

Lilian gazed out the window while Maddison finished the

call. The view from her corner office was breathtaking.

"I just wanted to congratulate you on getting the paperwork done." Maddison bowed in appreciation.

"Thank you, it was a journey," Lilian joked.

Lilian had been astonished at the state of the company's record keeping. If Maddison had been audited, they would have been fined. The level of non-compliance with basic accounting requirements was, at best, negligent.

"Also, I read your report, great initiative," Maddison commended.

Lilian had consulted Clarise on how to address Maddison's appalling bookkeeping. In Clarise's experience, clients didn't agree to pay for bad news, so she had instructed Lilian to prepare a report and Clarise would beg for forgiveness if required.

"I'm glad you found our advice insightful, there's a lot of work to be done," Lilian stated, not wanting to leave Maddison the impression rectification was optional.

"When you say our advice, do you mean my advice?" Maddison asked, wondering whether anyone else had contributed.

"I wrote the report myself," Lilian clarified, confused by the inference.

Maddison smiled at Lilian's modesty.

"Lilian, businesses pay a fortune for analysis of this quality. What on earth are you doing at Bondi Singh?" Maddison's attempt at a compliment was superbly demeaning.

"Maddison, my colleagues are just as capable."

"I doubt that, Lilian, but I admire your loyalty."

Lilian needed to check her watch but didn't want to offend Maddison, who was clearly not finished.

"The only thing your report doesn't include is, who should implement all your recommendations."

"Typically, a Chief Financial Officer or a Chief Operating Officer, or even yourself if you have the time," Lilian suggested, missing the subtext.

"Well, in that case, would you prefer to be a Chief Financial Officer or a Chief Operating Officer?" Maddison grinned.

Lilian was taken aback.

"I'm a tax lawyer. I don't have any experience implementing this level of change in an organisation of this size."

There was an eruption of laugher outside from Nabine's team, followed by a cheer.

"Have you noticed there are more staff in the office than when you started?" Maddison asked, smiling at the sound of her employees' merriment.

"There are more people here today than when I first started, comparatively," Lilian agreed, not grasping the relevance.

"They're here because you're here. They like coming into the office because you know what you're doing and they're learning new skills. You did that."

Lilian blushed.

"I know you have no formal experience in those roles, but given you were able to articulate with remarkable specificity what needs to be done and why, you would clearly be able to implement your own recommendations."

Maddison wanted Lilian and she wasn't going to take no for an answer.

"I need you because you make people want to work here. Take your time, think about your price and what resources you'll need."

Lilian was flattered by the offer, but her attention was split. She caved and looked at her watch.

"Sorry, Maddison. I need to get home. My husband is taking our nephew to the basketball tonight."

Maddison got up from her desk and walked to the window to watch the sky change colour, ignoring Lilian's goodbye.

"I know I should be embarrassed by your advice, but I'm so proud of what we built. The work we do here is special."

"What you do here is impressive, but I need to think about it," Lilian said, resisting Maddison's determination.

"I need someone I can trust with the management of the business. Our work is too important to fail," Maddison said with a hint of desperation.

"I've never considered becoming a manager, I'm a specialist." Lilian stood up with her briefcase.

"You're a natural leader. Henrietta told me you would probably have been running the Tax Office by now if you hadn't left."

"She was a great boss," Lilian said. She had high regard for Henrietta's opinion.

"And I trust her judgement. The job's yours if you want it. I hope you don't let insecurities stop you from accepting my offer."

Lilian consulted her watch, again. It was past time to leave. "I appreciate your faith, Maddison, I will think about it."

60

Lily had chosen gold as the theme for her eightieth birthday party. Her friends, clad in luminescent gowns and sequined tuxedos waited in line to hand Lily their presents.

She had refused her wheelchair and instead stayed seated at the table with Al by her side. Lily's nurse lingered, keeping a watchful eye on her client.

"Are you sure you don't want one of us to say something?" Lilian offered once the gift queue had dissipated, certain Lily would regret a party with no speeches.

"No, darling, but I would like to thank everyone for coming all this way for me. Do you think Coen might be able to rustle up a microphone?"

Al chuckled knowingly.

"I can find out," Lilian said.

"Thank you, darling. You look stunning," Lily remarked.

Lilian's tapered gold satin gown was on loan from Rachel.

A comrade from her bridge club cut in and captured Lily's attention so Lilian left the festivities in search of an amplifier.

She wandered the familiar hallways looking for Coen but she couldn't find him, so Lilian went to the kitchen.

She waited at the door for Brett to stop barking orders. Brett noticed his staff staring past his shoulder. "Hello, what do you need?"

"Lily has requested a microphone."

Brett joined Lilian in the hallway and stuck out a cheek to be pecked.

"There should be one upstairs, in the storeroom." Brett stood back and exaggeratedly considered Lilian's ensemble. "You look amazing tonight!"

"Thank you, see you later for cake." Lilian blushed then went to find the AV box.

By the time she got back to the Marina's makeshift ballroom, Lily was clutching a gold beaded microphone.

Coen spotted Lilian. "We had it decorated last week. Doug didn't believe Lily would get through the night without a song."

Lilian laughed. "I should have known you would be prepared."

"You look beautiful in that dress. Sydney is obviously working for you," Coen commented after a poorly disguised doubletake.

Apparently everyone thinks I look great except my husband, Lilian thought.

"Is this on?" Lily tapped the mouthpiece and feedback screeched across the room.

Guests abruptly stopped their conversations and began to gather around Lily's table.

Her grandchildren nestled at Lily's feet, her friends pulled up their chairs, and the rest stood in a cosy arch around the group.

Lilian was overcome by the sight of Lily sitting at the centre of the circle of love which had formed in her honour.

"It's a good thing my family have doubled since we were here for my seventieth, because half my friends have died."

The crowd laughed at the macabre joke.

"If you had told me then I would still be here for my eightieth, I never would have believed you. But I am still here, because of Al."

Family and friends cheered for Al.

"Darling, loving you every day has given me a reason to stay alive. I wouldn't have made it a day past seventy-five without you spoiling me as much as you can every day. And the greatest gift you have given me, is time. Without those five years, I would not have met these little cuddle pots."

Lily looked dotingly upon their newest additions.

Lilian shared Lily's gratitude that Dot and Beth had had the privilege of knowing their great-grandmother.

"Of course, my dear husband, you cannot take all the credit!"

Al laughed, having made no such claim.

"My one and only daughter, Dorothy, moved all the way to Melbourne to take care of me. And I don't think you expected me to live this long, did you, darling?"

Dorothy laughed at the jibe. No one had.

Lily collected her thoughts, emotion had fogged her spectacles.

"It would be remiss of me not to mention the loss we suffered this year. Yet another cruel loss for our family. While I'm still angry, I'm at peace in the knowledge the next loss you will endure will be my own." Her relatives groaned collectively. "And like so many of my late friends, who were so fortunate to make it to old age, my passing will be a celebration of my greatest achievement, you."

Lily's arm trembled under the weight of the dazzling microphone, and she handed it back to Coen.

Brett wheeled out a towering pyramid of eighty golden cupcakes as they sang Happy Birthday through bittersweet tears.

William snuck cupcakes for Dot and Beth and they sat on his knees lapping at shiny icing.

Lilian stood back and watched Al whispering with Lily. Marcus and Tim lifted Connie and Abbie off the floor while Ari hugged Jordan. Dorothy handed out cupcakes then brought one to Lilian.

"We're so lucky that everyone could get here for the party," Lilian said.

Dorothy sighed. "The next time we'll all be together, will be her funeral."

61

Rachel gripped Lilian's forearm and pushed through the bottleneck until they popped out the other side of the crowd.

"I thought this was supposed to be fun?" Lilian shouted over the music.

They headed away from the stage, towards the market.

"It is fun!" Rachel yelled, clapping Lilian on the back.

Lilian had appreciated the musicians but her desire to be at home outweighed her enjoyment of the performance.

"I'll take your word for it," Lilian joked, preferring to consume concerts from her living room.

"There's nothing like live music," Rachel replied. Now a local award winner, Rachel wanted to reciprocate the support.

"There is a nice vibe, and I'm looking forward to the parade," Lilian conceded, inspecting the indie stall offerings for gifts. Her daughters had been unimpressed they couldn't attend due to ironclad birthday party commitments.

"Thanks for coming, I know you hate festivals." Rachel squeezed Lilian's shoulder.

"I don't hate festivals. Getting separated, squashed, and sunburnt is just not my idea of fun. I do however like supporting our community," Lilian refuted, not wanting to defame others on account of her discomfort.

Rachel adored Lilian's uncompromising positivity. She knew Lilian truly hated festivals.

"Well, I'm glad you're here, so I can convince you to help me write my next book," Rachel admitted cheekily.

"What's this book about?"

They crossed the road to peruse the adjacent vendors.

"I haven't decided yet. What do you want to write about?" Rachel stopped to try on a hand-painted silk scarf.

While she waited for Rachel, Lilian browsed aimlessly through the racks. Hanging at the back of the marquee, Lilian spotted a robe almost identical to the one Lily had given her for her birthday. Tender memories came flooding back and a tear rolled down her cheek.

"Why are you crying?" Rachel asked, laughing nervously.

"I had a robe like this in Canberra. It reminded me of… the past," Lilian said. She had been about to say being in love but it felt disloyal.

"Happy tears?" Rachel checked, troubled by Lilian's reaction.

Lilian nodded. She wasn't unhappy with William, she had just forgotten what they had been like at the beginning.

"Well in that case." Rachel plucked the garment from her grasp.

Lilian watched while Rachel paid and begged her emotions to settle. Rachel handed Lilian the bag then led her to the food court.

They secured a free plastic picnic table, shaded by a tatty blue and white beach umbrella.

"I'll get us something refreshing," Rachel said, leaving Lilian to regroup.

It was a breezy spring day. The wind was cool, but the sun was boiling. Lilian relished the shade, and the break. She closed her eyes and filtered out the noise.

Rachel returned with two plastic cups, condensation dripping off the sides.

"Ice-cold homemade lemonade. It's delicious." Rachel sat, concerned about her friend. "So, do you want to talk about it?"

Lilian smiled, embarrassed. "Sorry, I don't know where that came from."

"I don't believe you," Rachel dismissed bluntly. "William?"

Lilian had no explanation for why the robe had provoked an outpouring of anguish.

"It just reminded me of how passionate we were in Canberra."

"Is everything okay at home?" Rachel asked, concealing her alarm.

It was a confronting question. Lilian wanted more than okay.

"I told William I wouldn't move back to Melbourne, and he didn't take it very well."

Rachel took a sip of her drink and waited for Lilian to continue.

"I doubt it would have occurred to him that I might refuse. William's never had to compromise, I don't think he knows how to deal with it."

Lilian watched the people bustling around her, she was more worried than she'd realised.

"How's he behaving?" Rachel asked.

"Nothing bad, he's just… sulking."

"I can't imagine it." Rachel frowned.

"I know, it's so unlike him. I think he feels betrayed, like me standing up for what's best for Dot and Beth means what he wants is less important?"

"What an idiot," Rachel said harshly.

Lilian laughed, touched by Rachel's fierce solidarity.

"Sorry, that was mean. I take it back," Rachel withdrew, still irritated.

"I forgive you," Lilian replied. "I'm just trying to give him some space so he can figure things out for himself."

Rachel pondered the situation, and concluded she had nothing insightful to add.

"Maybe your new robe will make him cry too?" Rachel joked.

Lilian laughed, almost choking on a lemony ice cube.

Rachel lay her calves over an empty chair and stretched into a sunbeam.

"Maybe." Lilian felt lighter. "Thanks for listening."

"You're welcome. What next? Parade, book planning or eat?" Rachel smiled, pleased to have been some help.

Lilian finished her drink.

"Eat, book planning, then parade?"

"Sounds like a plan," Rachel agreed. "I'm starving, lets walk and talk."

They snaked towards the food trucks, Rachel with one finger looped through the belt holder on Lilian's jeans.

"I'm glad you're on board with the next book," Rachel said hopefully when they reached the food court.

"I'm reserving my commitment until I know what it's about," Lilian corrected.

"Do you want to actually write this one or pretend and take the credit?" Rachel teased.

Lilian remembered a conversation with Carlos and wondered whether writing a book would push her soaring to new heights. "I'll think about it."

62

"Mummy, what's tax?" Beth had discovered if she evaded bedtime long enough, she might be awake when William got home from work.

"Good question!" Lilian lauded, stifling an exasperated groan.

"You know how we buy food because we need to eat every day?"

Beth nodded furiously.

"Well, tax is how we pay for things we only use sometimes, like the pool."

"Huh?" Beth moaned, perplexed.

Lilian tried a different approach, aware Beth didn't care about the answer.

"Tax is how we give money to people who need it more than us," Lilian rephrased, certain there was a better way to explain tax to a child.

"Like sharing is caring?" Beth proposed, glancing at the clock she couldn't read.

"Exactly, like that. You got it," Lilian replied, impressed. "Bedtime!"

Lighting fast, Lilian ceremoniously pulled the blanket up and tucked it under Beth.

"Nooooo." Beth squirmed, kicking the blankets away, cuteness replaced with steely determination.

"Sorry, its bedtime," Lilian sang while she retreated to the hall then switched off the light.

"Muuuuuuuuuuum!" Beth screeched.

Lilian closed the door on Beth standing defiantly on her mattress.

The wailing followed Lilian to the kitchen.

Dot was already in her bedroom. She preferred to hide from her sister in the evenings.

Lilian ordered dinner for William and herself, then studied the family diary and adjusted her lists accordingly.

Beth's resistance slowly weakened.

Lilian called Dorothy. "Hi, Mum. How are things there?"

"Hello, it was a good day today, only a few tears," Dorothy confirmed.

"I'm just trying to figure out what's happening over the next few months. Do you know how long you'll be staying in Sydney?"

Lilian could hear Ari speaking in the background.

"Ari wants to know if you could help her with some paperwork on the weekend?"

Lilian consulted the calendar which was so crammed with overlapping annotations she could barely read it.

"I'll find time, not sure when," Lilian promised, pleased to be asked to do something useful to support Ari.

She heard William open the front door.

"No plans to leave just yet. We do need to discuss Christmas at some point," Dorothy reminded Lilian.

They'd been putting off the conversation, unsure whether Lily or Ari would be well enough to travel.

William entered the kitchen carrying a large bouquet.

Lilian was immediately suspicious. "Mum, I'll call you tomorrow."

William placed the bundle on the bench and smiled.

"Flowers?" Lilian intimated a misdeed.

"They aren't for you, they're from a patient," William retorted.

Lilian noticed a strange tone in his voice. William seemed nervous.

"I've ordered take away. I was too busy to get to the supermarket." Lilian watched William unpack, waiting for an explanation for his mood.

"Well in that case, you will be very happy to know…" William inhaled sharply. "I quit!"

Lilian felt as though she'd been punched in the stomach.

"You quit what?" Lilian parroted, hoping she'd misunderstood.

"I quit my job, today." William's smile masked what Lilian could only assume was fear of her reaction.

"Why?" Lilian steadied herself against the counter.

"The board offered me a promotion. I knew if I took it, I would never leave. So I quit. I haven't written the letter yet, but it's done," William explained, trying to summon the crystal clarity which had possessed him earlier in the day.

Rage spread through Lilian's limbs and her breath slowed to a loud and deliberate hiss.

Lilian briefly moderated her fury to respond.

"I see what's going on here. I said no to Melbourne, and now you're just doing whatever you want in case I say no again."

William was shocked.

"I thought you'd be happy? We talked about this. You agreed

I need to spend more time at home."

"You thought I'd be happy you quit your job without discussing it with me first?" Lilian shouted quietly, mindful not to alert Dot or Beth to an argument.

William stared at her.

"Yes, I did. I thought you wanted to spend more time together?"

Lilian glared back.

"I have no idea who you are."

The comment froze them both. They stood paralysed, a chasm between them, each afraid to speak next.

The doorbell rang and Lilian broke away to collect their dinner.

When she returned to the kitchen William was slumped over the bench, eyes pooling with watery disbelief.

"I'm sorry," William's conviction dissipated.

Lilian took clean plates out of the dishwasher and placed them on the counter, then retrieved her car keys from the fruit bowl.

"I'm going for a drive, so I don't say something I regret," she advised hotly.

"Please don't drive while you're upset," William begged, distracted drivers a staple of his operating table.

The affection in his voice was agonising, affection she'd not heard recently.

Lilian threw her keys back in the bowl and headed outside to the salvation of the pavement.

The sun had set but the sky was still light.

Lilian walked to the beach. There were people milling about in their front yards, chatting, sipping wine, washing cars.

When she arrived at the foreshore, Lilian stopped to watch the waves. Dogs bounced around their owners' feet as they crossed the sand.

William was the person she used to turn to when the world made her feel this way, now he was the cause. Overwhelmed with despair, Lilian remembered her widowed sister and felt ashamed. At least her husband was still here.

63

"The issue, Mr Clarker, is that you don't understand input tax credits. If you did understand input tax credits, you wouldn't have claimed input tax credits on a Goods and Services Tax free supply. So, either you do understand input tax credits and you're a crook, or Mala rightly identified that you need help with input tax credits," Clarise surmised calmly.

"I agreed to be insulted personally, not professionally," Mr Clarker barked at Clarise as he leaned over her in the foyer, waiving a printout of Mala's advice.

Clarise stood up and crossed her arms. "Perhaps you should thank Mala for finding your error before you were charged, because you owe the Australian Tax Office over twenty thousand dollars!"

Mr Clarker tried to slam the memo on the counter but it anticlimactically slipped from his stubby fingers and fluttered to the floor. Further enraged at the paper's insolence, Mr Clarker stormed out.

"She's the best," Muhammad whispered to Lilian while they listened tensely.

The partition flew open and Clarise marched up the centre aisle into her office and slammed the door.

Muhammed cowered behind his screen and pretended to be working.

"I'll go," Lilian offered. She tapped lightly and called loudly, "Are you alright?"

Clarise stomped to the door and flung it open. "I cannot stand that fat little man! I knew we shouldn't have taken him on as a client. I had a bad feeling about him from the start. He's not worth the money."

Lilian tried not to laugh. It was unlike Clarise to get angry over someone so unreasonable.

"You might get your wish. It didn't sound like he'll be back." Lilian's attempt at humour failed to defuse her boss.

"Sorry, Lilian. I'm so mad. Mala's work was exceptional, and his response was to rubbish her reputation. Honestly, how hard is it for people to just say thank you?" Clarise vented.

Lilian was endlessly surprised when clients asked for their expertise but struggled to accept their findings.

"You did a great job out there. Mala is lucky to have you standing up for her," Lilian commended.

Clarise let out a therapeutic groan and unwound slightly.

"I would prefer it if we didn't have clients like that at all," Clarise said, too incensed to recognise a compliment.

Satisfied Clarise was debriefed, Lilian got up to leave.

"I have been waiting for your resignation letter," Clarise blurted.

Lilian was baffled by the comment. "Because of Mr Clarker?"

Clarise shook her head and laughed. "Maddison admitted she offered you a job. I think she felt guilty."

"You put a clause in her contract saying she can't poach me," Lilian reminded Clarise.

"Don't worry about that," Clarise assured Lilian, abashed by her selfish prowess.

So often conversations with Clarise felt like an ambush.

"I haven't thought about it. It's not great timing," Lilian replied, uncomfortable with the encouragement.

"Are you sure? That kind of opportunity doesn't come around every day and things aren't going to change here," Clarise remarked. The line between employer and friend had always been murky.

"Thanks for your concern, Clarise. I will make a decision when I'm ready." Lilian was beginning to feel pressured, she didn't appreciate being lectured.

Clarise nodded, sensing she'd crossed a boundary, and Lilian returned to her desk.

Mala and Murph were back from their appointment and Muhammed had updated them on Clarise's battle with Mr Clarker.

"Is Clarise okay?" Mala pouted, upset her work had caused an altercation.

"Clarise is fine, everyone back to work," Lilian said, dispersing the gossips.

Just as her colleagues had finally settled down, Jason shot out of his office.

"Lil, let's get a coffee," Jason said and then went outside.

Lilian grabbed her bag and followed.

"Clarise says you're not resigning?" Jason stated, no attempt to conceal his source.

"Clarise should not repeat confidential conversations."

Jason ignored the criticism, they all lived in each other's pockets. "Is this because William quit the hospital?"

Lilian had forgotten Jason and William surfed together most mornings.

"It's none of your business, Jason."

"Maybe not, Lilian, but your husband doesn't know Maddison offered you a job because he would have told me. So what's going on with you two?"

Lilian felt like she'd been slapped. She was angry and too embarrassed to speak.

"Maybe William wouldn't have quit if he'd known. He would be devastated if his actions stopped you from accepting a once-in-a-lifetime opportunity," Jason said in defence of his good friend.

Lilian was nauseous with rage.

"This. Is. None. Of. Your. Business!" Lilian shouted, hoping Jason would listen if she yelled it the second time.

Shoppers on the other side of the road had gathered to watch the argument.

"It is my business, Lilian. You lied to him and now I'm stuck in the middle."

Lilian felt bad. Jason was not innately nosy, unlike his staff.

"What are you implying, Jason? I tell William or you will?" Lilian was about to cry, mostly from shame.

"I'm not going to tell anyone anything. I'm just worried about you, both," Jason replied softly.

"I'm going back to work." Humiliated, Lilian walked off.

Instead of going back into the office, she sat in her car until the end of the workday, crying her way through a box of tissues.

Muhammed knocked on the window on his way past.

"Why are you sitting in the car?" he asked, clearly unaware of her fight with Jason.

Lilian hid the emotional turmoil still churning and lowered her window. "I'm fine. I'm just thinking."

64

Dot and Jordan flanked Beth as they strolled through the zoo. Beth, terrified by the animals, clung to her protective guard. Behind, William and Juan were deep in conversation, Connie asleep over William's shoulder and Abbie draped over Juan.

"Juan's great. It's a pity you took so long to introduce us," Ari said to Dorothy who'd crumpled under the pressure to produce her new boyfriend.

"We thought you were hiding him because he was sketchy," Lilian admitted.

Dorothy smiled.

"Or you met him somewhere dodgy?" Ari prodded.

Dorothy laughed, regretting that her family knew nothing about her relationship with Juan.

"Juan's a professor, he specialises in art history," Dorothy said, spoiling the speculation with the unsensational truth.

Ari and Lilian shared an impressed glance.

"So sophisticated," Ari remarked, disappointed.

William stopped to make sure Lilian was following them around the corner before he disappeared with Beth towards the hippo enclosure.

"If he's totally respectable, then why all the secrecy?" Lilian understood Dorothy not wanting Juan to know she was a widow, but she didn't have to keep her daughters in the dark.

"You're one to talk," Ari teased.

"This isn't about me," Lilian chided.

"We met while he was separated. I didn't want to encourage anything while he was trying to work things out with his wife. He'd only been divorced a few months when he asked me out, so I tried to keep things casual because I wasn't sure if he was really over her," Dorothy explained.

Lilian quickened her pace, reflexively anxious when Dot and Beth were out of view.

"And now?" Lilian asked.

Dorothy sighed. "Now I'm in a quandary. I was never planning on staying in Melbourne."

"You don't have to come back to Sydney," Ari said.

"I could stay in Melbourne, but I want to be with the family."

Her daughters reappeared in Lilian's eyeline, and the instinctual worry abated.

"It's endless. Everyone shuffling around. Someone always has to compromise," Lilian mused rhetorically.

"Juan knows if he wants to be with me long term, he will need to move. My future is in Sydney."

"What if we decided to go back to Melbourne?" Lilian wagered.

Dorothy was surprised by the question. She hadn't considered the possibility.

"Are you thinking about going back?" Ari blurted, alarmed.

William and Juan had taken a seat in the gallery while Beth pressed her forehead against the glass, unintentionally baiting the hippo.

"No, but you never know," Lilian speculated, curious as to Dorothy's conviction.

William waved at Lilian, indicating for their group to follow Dot and Jordan, who had veered toward the platypi.

"Well, it certainly makes the decision easier with you both in Sydney," Dorothy replied.

Ari was rattled by Lilian's open-mindedness.

"Why are you thinking about going back to Melbourne? I thought that was settled?" Ari panicked at the thought of being separated from both her mother and sister.

"I'm not leaving, but this is never going to end. It will be family all over the place for the rest of our lives. We will always be separated from someone. Even if we're all here, William's family are in Melbourne," Lilian reminded Ari.

They sighed, acknowledging the cost of their own proximity, grateful to be together.

"Have you told William about your job offers yet?" Ari asked.

"I thought we were talking about Juan?" Lilian deflected.

Dorothy laughed, glad to be out from under the microscope. "Why didn't you tell William in the first place?"

Lilian had found that answer during her afternoon stewing in the car, confronting her compounding deceptions.

"I didn't want to give him an excuse to convince me to go back to Melbourne."

Ari shrugged, not grasping the correlation.

"Tom was so unwell. I was afraid that if William thought I was considering changing jobs, he would guilt trip me into leaving. Clarise offered me a directorship, and then Rachel asked me to write a book, and then Maddison asked me to stay, and the omissions just snowballed and I didn't know where to start. It's not William's fault I didn't have the courage to stand up for myself."

Dorothy hugged Lilian, proud of her daughter's self-awareness. "It must have felt very lonely not being able to talk to William."

The hippo had begun plodding toward the window and Beth had started convulsing with fear. William left Connie with Juan and went to save Beth.

Juan was out of his depth and called Ari over to corral her twins.

"I'm sorry you were suffering with this alone," Dorothy added, realising she had been so consumed with Ari and Lily she hadn't noticed Lilian had been struggling.

Lilian was touched by her mother's humility.

"Honestly, I wasn't even thinking about myself. I was just focused on the girls. I kept telling everyone I would think about things and then never put in the effort."

"You're being way too hard on yourself," Dorothy said tenderly.

Dot and Jordan were back with William supporting Beth to confront the hippo now snuggling up to the glass.

"No, Mum, I haven't been hard enough. I was just drifting, and I used to know better." Lilian appreciated her mother's bottomless compassion, but Lilian knew Dorothy was wrong.

Ari bounced the twins on her knees while they squealed delightfully at the hippo playing with Beth.

"Now William's at home all the time trying to decide what he wants to do next, and we're not talking about it together," Lilian confessed, ashamed by the state of her marriage.

"Do you know what you want to do next?" Dorothy asked.

Lilian finally felt in control. "I do, but I want to talk to my husband about it first."

65

Lilian visited her old bedroom at the terrace while Lily was with her nurse. Dorothy had converted it into a sitting room years ago. Vines had grown up from the courtyard and now covered the bricks outside the window. Lilian recognised nothing, her stint at the terrace had been erased.

She heard the nurse close the front door on her way out and returned to the living room.

"Sorry, darling. They're very stubborn," Lily apologised for the interruption, unmoved from her armchair.

"No problem, I think you mean thorough," Lilian teased light-heartedly.

The homecare nurses had been excellent. Lilian wished they'd engaged them sooner, even though she knew Lily would never have agreed.

"Darling, it's a bit chilly." Lily shivered. Her aged vocal cords made her sound perpetually cranky.

Lilian closed the sliding door. She noticed their table and chairs had been sown in place by weeds.

Lily's decline had been gradual, but it was confronting for Lilian. She hadn't known Lily now used a frame to walk around inside the house.

"How's Al?" Lilian enquired.

"I didn't ask you to fly to Melbourne to talk about my husband," Lily rebuffed.

Lilian had been concerned when Lily had summoned her and Al had had no idea why. Al's intel was usually more reliable.

"What did you want to talk about?" Lilian replied, impatient to discover what was so important it required a conversation in person.

"I want you to look me in the eye and tell me you don't still believe in that silly curse," Lily challenged.

Of all the reasons Lilian had pondered on the plane, the curse had not made the cut.

"No one has mentioned the curse in a decade, let alone since Carlos died." Lilian's attempt at nonchalance was unconvincing.

"That's not an answer," Lily chided. She knew her granddaughter too well.

Lilian didn't want to admit it, and be told she was foolish, but it was wasted breath to attempt to deceive Lily.

"Fine. It's crossed my mind," Lilian confessed.

Lily scowled at her.

"Lilian, this nonsense must stop. You cannot allow your little girls to grow up in fear of falling in love, as you did."

Lilian was offended. "I would never burden my girls. My worries are my own."

Lily waggled her finger.

"And what about William? Are you going to spend the rest of your life refusing to let him climb ladders or get a dog?" Lily's tone softened. She had not asked Lilian to Melbourne intending to scold her.

Lilian had thought her secret battle with fate had gone unnoticed, but Lily had picked up on her subtle precautions.

Lilian stood up and paced, insulted by the accusation, but she knew Lily was right.

"Don't deny it. This needs to stop!" Lily demanded.

Lilian flopped back onto the couch.

"I'm not denying it," she conceded.

To avoid Lily's judgement, Lilian focused on the glossy green spring leaves whirling around the courtyard.

"You can't live your life worrying about what might happen next," Lily counselled sympathetically.

Lilian's tea was tepid. She went to boil the kettle, tired of being bombarded by other people's opinions of her life.

"I don't sit around all day terrified something awful will happen," Lilian refuted, conscious she might if she wasn't so busy.

Lilian prepared a fresh pot and returned to the couch.

"You can't wrap your family in cotton wool, especially if they don't know you're doing it." Lily's deduction sounded harsher than she'd intended.

"I'm not locking the kids in the house and never letting them out," Lilian replied defensively.

Lily took a biscuit.

"And Beth hates dogs." *Thankfully*, Lilian thought.

"Your family are entitled to take risks and you shouldn't intervene because of a curse that isn't real, that's all," Lily finished, content she'd aired her concerns.

"I don't believe in the curse and I'm not arbitrarily detaining my family," Lilian assured her.

She patted Lily's knee, appreciative her grandmother cared enough to force a ridiculous conversation.

Depleted from the confrontation, Lily sipped her tea.

Lilian was relieved the inquisition was over.

"We couldn't have done this over the phone?" she joked.

"That's not why I asked you to come. Can you pass me my walker?"

The nurse had moved the frame next to the fireplace. Lilian wheeled it over to Lily.

When Lily tried to stand, the tremors in her hands exposed her fragility. Lilian gently supported Lily's weight as she pulled herself up from the chair.

"Can I help?"

"Stop fussing," Lily refused then slowly made her way to the bedroom.

Obediently, Lilian stayed on the couch, listening to Lily shuffle along the floorboards.

Lilian admired the courtyard garden as she waited. It was overgrown from Dorothy's extended absence. She was reminded of peaceful mornings pressed against the warm brick.

Lily wheeled back into the living room with a carved wooden box resting on the seat of her walker.

Lilian's heart was in her throat. "Your jewellery?"

"Yes, darling."

Lilian wanted to accuse Lily of being sensational, but she couldn't find words to speak.

Reversing herself into position in front of the armchair, Lily collapsed safely back onto the cushions, then nudged the walker towards her.

Lilian picked up the box.

"I need to show you who will get which piece. The rest of my wishes are in my will," Lily explained, closing her eyes, exhausted from the exertion.

Lilian fought the implication. Lily had never spoken of her death, unless in jest.

"You could live for years yet, Lily. This is unnecessary," Lilian argued. Eighty was young these days.

Lily reached out to console her granddaughter. Lilian kissed her hand, wishing Lily couldn't see her tears.

Lily sighed. "Darling, this body does not agree with you."

66

Lilian and Alloysius had spent the afternoon painstakingly reviewing correspondence to check for non-compliance. Dion had appeared sporadically with sustenance and messages of moral support from Maddison.

"Great work today." Lilian closed her laptop with a broad smile.

Alloysius marvelled at her boundless energy. "I don't know whether I'm not very good at this, or you're just exceptional?"

"You're a generalist, I'm a specialist. You aren't expected to know this level of detail," Lilian reassured him.

"You're too kind. You really are remarkable," Alloysius gushed.

Lilian ignored the compliment.

"How did you get into tax?" Alloysius wondered what would draw someone so enigmatic to specialise in a field so dull.

Lilian had picked up her laptop to leave and placed it back on the boardroom table.

"I fell in love with it at law school," Lilian reminisced. "Tax is fascinating. I enjoy the nuance between what policy makers are seeking to achieve when they make laws and the reality of how the law is implemented."

Alloysius swooned. "No wonder the Tax Office didn't want to let you go. They should have put you on a poster!"

Lilian laughed, picking up her laptop again. Alloysius wasn't finished.

"What do you enjoy more, law or tax?"

Lilian put down her laptop, again.

"It's like you're asking me to pick a favourite child," Lilian joked.

Dion poked his head around the door. "All right in here?"

"We've just finished," Alloysius confirmed, grinning proudly.

"Go team!" Dion punched the air, then disappeared.

Alloysius waited for Lilian's response to his insightful question.

"I would have to say tax," Lilian concluded. "The law is a tool. I like the way tax reflects society."

Alloysius was mesmerised. "Why?"

Lilian wondered whether her colleague needed to get home to his wife. She grabbed her computer and started to edge towards the door.

"For example, a century ago politicians considered applying a bachelor's tax to men who refused to marry unattractive women." Lilian smiled. It was one of her favourite tax trivia questions. "Tax changes when we change, it reflects what we value."

"How ludicrous. What percentage of income?"

Lilian laughed. "I don't know, I never asked."

She had made it to the door, with half a leg in the hall.

"Have a good night, Lilian. As always, it was a pleasure working with you today." Alloysius blushed, realising at last that Lilian was trying to end the meeting.

"Good night," Lilian called as she sprinted back to her office and packed up.

Maddison was standing at the window when Lilian tapped on the door and broke her concentration.

"Have you got a minute?" Lilian asked.

"Sure, I was just brainstorming," Maddison said, moving to her couch.

Lilian sat at the desk to avoid the light reflecting off the harbour.

"How did things go today?" Maddison enquired.

"Very well. We're finished with the damage control. It should be smooth sailing from here on," Lilian updated.

"Does that mean your assignment with us is at an end?" Maddison pre-empted, suspicious of Lilian's impromptu visit.

"It means you won't need me at the office every day. Alloysius and Nabine can call me anytime if they need a consultation," Lilian promised.

Maddison tapped her fingers apprehensively on the arm of the couch.

"I wanted to let you know in person, I considered your offer and have decided to decline," Lilian advised. Maddison didn't need coddling.

Lilian braced to hold her ground. Maddison sprung up and sat opposite Lilian at the desk.

"How much to convince you to stay?" Maddison demanded fiercely, not amenable to rejection.

Lilian didn't expect Maddison to be happy, but she was surprised Maddison thought she could be bought.

"This isn't about money. Just because I can do the job, doesn't mean it's what I want."

Lilian missed her tax chats with her colleagues at Bondi Singh.

Maddison wasn't ready to concede. "So, what do you want?"

Lilian felt herself getting irritated. Maddison wasn't listening.

"Maddison, thank you for the opportunity. I feel valued and appreciated here, and I adore the staff but I love working exclusively on tax law matters. Sorry, I'm not interested."

Maddison crossed her arms. "I don't want to lose you."

Lilian smiled apologetically. "I'm not yours to lose."

Maddison stood and walked back to the window.

"Well at least you will still be a phone call away when we need you."

The glare was making Lilian nauseous.

Maddison sighed. "You're going to have to tell Nabine. She's going to be distraught."

Lilian laughed, relieved her message had finally been received.

"I'm so thankful for your offer. I want you to know how invigorating it has been working for you," Lilian told Maddison heartfully.

"Lilian, I should be thanking you. You revived this office, this team believes in themselves again," Maddison said emotionally, frustrated she had nothing to offer Lilian that would convince her to stay.

"I'm glad I was able to help," Lilian replied and hugged Maddison, then went back to her office and collected her briefcase.

On her way out, Lilian placed her pass on Dion's desk. Maddison had her answer, and it was time to move on.

67

Ari and Lilian sat at the back of the theatre, engrossed in Jordan's ballet rehearsal. Jordan seemed tiny against the older dancers but he kept pace and, as far as Lilian could tell, never faltered.

Ari had become overwhelmed and wanted to go for a walk during the interval.

"How are you feeling?" Lilian asked, concerned.

"Not sure?" Ari shook her arms like she was trying to wake from a bad dream.

Lilian stopped to peer through a boutique window at the designers on display.

"I can drop Jordan home, if you want to leave?" Lilian offered.

"Thanks, I think I'll be able to make it through. I want to see the second act," Ari said shakily, appreciative of her family's endless patience.

Lilian checked the opening times on the shop door, she needed some new shirts.

Ari noticed Lilian rubbing her sore hand.

"I broke your wrist!" Ari gasped, cradling Lilian's hand to inspect the damage.

Ari's grip had been so tight, Lilian had lost all sensation in her fingers. Lilian had given up trying to understand the manifestations of Ari's grief and valiantly tolerated her sister's need to crush her hand.

"That's okay, my husband's a surgeon. Sorry, was a surgeon, although I assume he still remembers how to bandage broken fingers."

Lilian pulled her hand to safety, wishing she'd not used the word husband while Ari was distressed.

"Enough about me, why were you squeezing my hand?"

Ari shuddered. "I was just thinking about how my husband will never know his son is a ballet prodigy. That morphed into, why couldn't Dot have had a ballet party last year, then Jordan would have discovered ballet before he…" Ari's voice began to quake.

Bargaining, Lilian thought. Textbook grief.

"I know it's bargaining," Ari commented in response to Lilian's expression.

"I didn't say anything." Lilian laughed.

"Anyway, it's like that with everything. Same with the twins, so many firsts, so many new traits about them he would have loved."

"Are you alright?" Lilian began to worry. Ari's mood could instantly slip into despair.

"No, but there's nothing I can do about it," Ari resolved stoically.

Lilian noticed the other parents mulling about the stage door. "We should head back."

Ari paused, accepted her pain, then stabilised and started walking.

"How are things with William at home?" Ari asked, seeking a distraction.

Lilian seriously doubted marriage was a wise choice of topic. "You really want me to talk about my husband?"

Ari laughed at Lilian's awkward attempt not to upset her.

"Of course, our lives haven't stopped. William has worked all day every day since you two started dating, it must be weird for you to have him at home?" Ari wrapped her arm around Lilian's waist.

They had arrived at the entrance to the community theatre too early to be let back inside.

Lilian pondered how her life had changed. The girls were deliriously happy. "I'm eating a lot."

Ari laughed. "Not what I was expecting you to say. Why are you eating a lot?"

The theatre reopened and the ballet parents inspected Ari and Lilian as they passed, curious about the genealogy of the new superstar outshining their children.

"William's cooking all day. Three course meals for dinner, dropping gourmet lunches off at the office, baking muffins for after school," Lilian explained, not sure why she felt self-conscious.

"He must be missing surgery. He needs something to do with his hands," Ari deduced. "Can I get in on this?"

Lilian laughed. "You're welcome to borrow him for the weekend."

"Does he know what he wants to do yet?" Ari asked, feeling hungry.

"He's been helping Tom with some medical research, but other than that, he's just surfing, cooking, and playing with the girls all day."

The last of the audience had trickled inside and they returned to their seats in the back row.

"Have you two talked about when William's going to get a job?"

A fellow ballet parent interjected to congratulate Ari on Jordan's talent.

The lights dimmed and the admirer scurried back to the front row.

"Have you decided what you want to do?" Lilian redirected before Ari could repeat her question.

"I don't like to admit it when you're right but I don't want to run Mum's business. It's not my thing, it was just convenient."

Lilian was intrigued. "What's your thing?"

Ari sighed. "I don't know. Look at my inspirational son, his calling found him. Maybe my passion will fall in my lap at a birthday party."

A clan of mothers were brazenly pointing at Ari and whispering, making no attempt to conceal their gossiping about Jordan.

Lilian grimaced. "I don't know how many more birthday parties I can take."

"I don't remember going to a million birthday parties when we were kids?" Ari stretched her memory.

"It's a nice idea though, your passion finding you," Lilian said as the curtain crept open, and the crowd quietened.

Jordan floated to his starting position, oblivious to the attention he'd garnered during the break.

Ari sucked in a sharp breath, preparing for the agony. Lilian reached for her sister's hand, ready to share her pain.

68

"You look exquisite." William kissed Lilian on the cheek, careful to avoid her lipstick, then rang Rachel's doorbell.

Lilian blushed.

William seemed to have decided it was now his fulltime job to seduce his wife. Mornings were filled with cute notes, heart shaped cookies and poems, leading to leisurely afternoons making love while she was supposed to be working from home. Lilian chose to savour the romance renaissance, aware William's attention would dissipate when he re-joined society.

"Sorry we're late," Lilian pleaded as Charlie opened the door.

"Happy Birthday," William added, handing Charlie a bottle of champagne and a card.

"Aww, thank you. Come in, sweeties." Charlie kissed them both, twice, and took their coats.

The dinner guests were already seated. Rachel was in the kitchen plating up catered entrées.

Two unclaimed seats remained, diagonally opposite in the middle of the table.

William apologised as he squeezed between strangers and the wall.

"Everyone, this is Lilian and William," Charlie announced over the chatter, then left to assist her fiancé.

Lilian peered around the table, eight faces she didn't recognise. Lilian wasn't surprised, she was rarely invited to events requiring a partner as William had notoriously never been available.

Charlie's friends considered the unfamiliar additions to their inner circle. William and Lilian had recently been elevated in Charlie estimates, now Rachel had secured Lilian as her matron of honour.

"I'm Lilian, this my husband, William," Lilian repeated.

Each friend echoed an obligatory polite hello, then returned to their discussions.

The woman seated to Lilian's left, opposite William, appeared thrilled with fresh dinner company.

"I'm Miriam, I work with Charlie," she shared eagerly.

"Hi, Miriam. I worked with Rachel on her last book." Lilian provided her credentials, appreciative of the warm reception.

William had found a willing conversationalist to his right and had turned away.

"That's exciting. You're an author," Miriam remarked, impressed.

"Rachel's the author, I'm a tax lawyer. Our book was about finances," Lilian corrected.

"Well, as long as you're happy," Miriam jibed, visibly disappointed.

"Rachel has been trying to talk me into writing another book, so maybe I should start telling people I'm a tax lawyer and an author," Lilian said, trying to salvage her status.

Miriam perked up. "What are you two planning for the next one?"

"Actually, I've been thinking about writing a book on my own about the history of tax policy." Lilian voiced the idea for the first time out loud.

William spun around and interjected before Miriam could reply. "You've started writing a book?"

"No, I was just telling Miriam I've been thinking about maybe writing a book about tax," Lilian replied, surprised by his tone.

Having lost interest in Lilian, Miriam turned to William. "And what do you do, William?"

William glared at Lilian. "I used to be a surgeon, but I left the profession to spend more time with my daughters."

Our daughters, Lilian thought.

"That's wonderful, what an amazing father." Miriam clasped her hands together with admiration and turned back to Lilian. "You must feel very lucky to have such a devoted husband."

Lilian nodded, tempted to spoil Miriam's delusion.

"What do you do these days, when you aren't caring for the children?" Miriam asked William.

"Actually, I'm moving down to Melbourne for a few months to take care of my father. He's been extremely unwell."

Lilian nearly choked on a mouthful of soda water.

Rachel emerged from the kitchen, clad performatively in a pristine apron.

"For entrées, we have asparagus tartlet and scallops," Rachel projected and began placing giant plates with tiny portions on the placemats.

"I'm so sorry to hear your father is poorly. You must be awfully worried," Miriam sympathised, unaware Lilian had been shocked into silence.

"I am, Miriam, thank you. We lost my mother last year, so we're all just pitching in to keep him afloat," William divulged, fishing for reinforcement.

Rachel placed a plate in front of Lilian and then Miriam. "Hello, you two."

"Rachel, William was just telling Miriam how he's going to live in Melbourne for a few months," Lilian relayed flatly.

Rachel didn't miss a beat.

"That's great. Lilian, can you please give me a hand with these plates? The entrees are getting cold," Rachel responded, equally devoid of emotion.

Lilian followed Rachel to the kitchen. Rachel made sure the door was completely sealed, fearing Lilian was about to scream.

"Did my husband just tell a stranger he's moving to Melbourne for a few months?" Lilian seethed.

Rachel winced. "I wasn't there, but it would appear that is what happened."

Lilian placed her hand on her heart, her chest felt like it might explode.

"I think I'm having a heart attack," Lilian said, numbness spreading.

"Stay there, I do actually need to deliver the rest of the entrées." Rachel quickly poured Lilian a glass of cold sparking water and propped her against the fridge.

Lilian hid in the kitchen while Rachel made two more trips.

After all the servings had been delivered, Rachel returned. "How do you want play this?"

Lilian sipped the icy drink, hoping it would soothe her rage.

"If you want to start a fight at the table, I'm fine with that," Rachel said supportively.

Lilian laughed, humour helped.

"Thanks, I'm okay. I can get through dinner," she vowed, determined not to ruin Charlie's birthday.

"Deep breaths!" Rachel steered Lilian back to the dining table before she could change her mind.

Lilian took her seat. William was chatting and eating, oblivious to her extended absence.

Miriam munched on a sourdough roll. "William was just telling me he's a surfer. Do you surf too?"

"I'm usually at home with our kids." Lilian picked up the entrée fork and poked her tartlet.

"Lilian is a great mother. We're very lucky," William sapped.

"What a charming family," Miriam remarked.

Lilian was nauseated by the front. "Yes, his girls will miss him while he's gone."

69

Dorothy paid for their oranges while Lilian plucked snow peas from a farm crate.

Frenzied marketeers hunting the best produce were bumping into each other, one knocking Lilian and their trolley into the back of a trailer.

"Hey!" Lilian cried, glancing at Dorothy for sympathy.

"You want the best, you've got to fight for it," Dorothy retorted.

Lilian was content with edible if it meant not getting trampled at dawn.

Dorothy paid for the snow peas, unfazed by the hustle.

"I need a break," Lilian complained, rubbing her battered hip.

"Let's stop for a coffee," Dorothy suggested, and they veered toward the bakery cart.

Dorothy ordered lattes while Lilian found a spare haybale, then they sat amongst the other locals waiting for their liquid motivation.

"What time is William's flight?" Dorothy asked.

"Late tonight, he wants to spend the day with the girls."

Dorothy bit her tongue, but Lilian caught the flicker of disapproval.

"What?" Lilian prodded.

"I'm not getting involved."

"You obviously have an opinion," Lilian snapped.

"I don't," Dorothy denied, again betrayed by her expressive features.

A fight broke out at the end of the lot in front of an olive loaf van.

Lilian crossed her arms and glared at Dorothy.

"I'm just surprised, I didn't think William would go through with leaving," Dorothy censored.

"Why are you surprised? He wants to spend time with Tom."

Dorothy cursed being trapped in a coffee queue, unable to escape, and patted Lilian's knee. "I appreciate William has a noble reason, I just think it's naive of him to expect you to be waiting for him when he gets back."

"Are you implying my marriage is so fickle we can't withstand a couple of months apart?" Lilian erupted, offended by the insinuation.

Dorothy groaned, unable to avoid explaining the obvious to her unassuming daughter.

"No, I'm not implying that at all. Partners grow apart when they aren't together. You're gorgeous and brilliant. Your husband has just proved he can't compromise and he's willing to leave his children."

Lilian was gutted by her mother's crass oversimplification.

"William wants to spend time with Tom and I'm not going anywhere," she rebutted.

Dorothy felt desperately sad. "No one plans for their relationship to fall apart."

Lilian was sick of being lectured.

"I'm going to get the lettuce." Lilian marched away, leaving Dorothy with the trolley to watch for their coffees.

Lilian wandered mindlessly between the trailers, resenting Dorothy for applying her bitter generalisations to Lilian's circumstances.

Remembering she was supposed to be looking for lettuce, she bought the least perilous bunch and returned to Dorothy who was waiting patiently with two steaming paper cups.

"I'm not angry," Lilian stated and took her latte.

"I should hope not, given I haven't done anything," Dorothy responded coolly.

Lilian conceded. Her mother was only sharing her perspective at Lilian's insistence, but Lilian was still annoyed.

"You think my husband takes our marriage for granted?" Lilian stoked.

Dorothy sipped her coffee.

"I don't. I think he's just focused on Tom and hasn't considered that you might meet someone better. I don't mean that as a criticism."

Lilian tried to expand her mind, she trusted Dorothy's instincts. "I honestly can't envisage any situation where I would leave him."

"William is about to trundle off to Melbourne mid career change. You mightn't recognise the person who comes back claiming to be your husband."

Lilian was reminded of her own words to William on the night he'd resigned sans discussion.

"I don't want to visualise my marriage failing." Lilian,

unsettled by the sensation, was done with the coffee and the conversation. "What's next?"

Exonerated, Dorothy smiled and consulted the list. "Tomatoes and bok choy."

Replenished, they resumed the battle.

"How's Juan?" Lilian asked.

Dorothy hesitated. "He's well."

Lilian secured an unguarded tray of plump cherry tomatoes.

"Juan asked me to marry him."

Lilian almost dropped the punnets.

"And you're telling me this now!" Lilian was horrified that she'd talked about herself all morning.

"It's not a big deal. He found an apartment in Sydney and asked me if I wanted to buy it together and get married," Dorothy said, downplaying the pragmatic proposal.

"What did you say?" Lilian was baffled by Dorothy's nonchalance.

"I said I would think about it," Dorothy confirmed indifferently.

"Why? You're completely in love."

Dorothy squeezed into a narrow gap between two vendors and retrieved as much bok choy as she could grab, conscious of Lilian making a scene.

"I don't want to flaunt my engagement in front of my grieving daughter and dying mother," Dorothy justified quietly, her tiredness visible.

"So, you said yes?" Lilian was confused.

"No, I said I would consider moving in with him and we could talk about marriage and property ownership later on if we're happy living together." Dorothy paid for their vegetables.

"Don't put this on Lily and Ari. They would be furious if they knew you were delaying marrying Juan because of them."

Dorothy was still living at Ari's apartment.

"It's not just because of them. I'm not in a hurry to make another lifelong commitment."

"Ari would want you to be happy, you have to tell her," Lilian insisted, dreading her sister's reaction to more deception from Dorothy.

"And say what? I know you can barely function but I'm leaving you to move in with my boyfriend." Dorothy sighed. Her family would always be her priority. "Juan knows I have responsibilities."

Lilian wished her mother would heed her own advice. "Juan won't wait forever!"

70

Lilian cubed a block of cheese then added the squares to a platter of apple, strawberries and watermelon.

"Your daughters feast like queens," Jason commended as he entered the office kitchen to make his afternoon cup of green tea.

Reaching over Lilian, Jason helped himself to a slice of apple.

"That they do," Lilian agreed, pinching a strawberry.

"I'm on your side, you know," Jason assured her.

Lilian was touched, Jason only ever aligned himself on principle. "There are no sides, Jason, but that's very kind of you."

"No need to thank me. Only a foolish man makes himself redundant in his own home," Jason stated. "See you tomorrow."

Jason had taken to barricading himself in his office to avoid being cuddled by Min and Dot after school.

Lilian finished the fruits, took two juice boxes out the fridge then returned to her desk.

Clarise had returned with their ballerinas.

Resolved to compensate for her father's absence, Murph and Mala took extra care to ask Dot about her day.

Lilian picked up the phone to check on Beth.

"Hi, Mum, all good there?" Lilian could hear the television in the background.

"Hello. Yes, Beth says to tell you she painted a butterfly for you at kinder and she's going to draw another butterfly now to give to Dot," Dorothy relayed Beth's message in her grandmotherly tone.

Lilian smiled, imagining Beth grinning proudly. Apparently William was unworthy of a butterfly.

Dot went to greet Muhammad.

"Thanks, Mum. See you later," Lilian replied and hung up.

Lilian watched Dot bask in the attention of her colleagues and pondered Jason's observation.

Dorothy cooked dinner every night, then they all ate together at Ari's apartment. By the time Lilian got her daughters back to their house, they bathed then went straight to bed. Lilian and William's once bustling family home now served as a changing room. William was superfluous to their new routine.

Dot finished with Yael then rushed to give Lilian a hug.

"How was school?" Lilian snuggled her eldest.

"I got a new reader, we had sport, and I fell over at lunch but I didn't hurt myself," Dot repeated for the fifth time, pointing to a swollen red knee.

"That's great! There are snacks in the back," Lilian prompted, irritated Dot's father wasn't around to provide medical care.

Once Dot and Min had retreated to the kitchen, Lilian returned a call from Nabine to discuss calculating Fringe Benefits Tax.

Clarise appeared in her doorway and summoned Lilian to her office.

Lilian finished the call and went to see Clarise. "Everything alright?"

Clarise looked guilty.

"I have prepared a bribe," she announced and pulled an envelope out of her desk drawer and handed it to Lilian.

"What am I being bribed to do?" Lilian was amused and curious to hear what task was so unappetising it required coercion.

She unsealed the tab. It contained a family pass to the local adventure playground.

"I need you to take Mr Clarker from Mala," Clarise blurted, then hurriedly lifted a notebook to shield her face from a pelting.

Lilian laughed, Clarise was hilarious.

"You don't need to bribe me to do my job." Lilian slid the envelope back across the table.

"He's so awful, Lilian. You're the only one who's going to be able to handle him," Clarise pleaded, handing the incentive back to Lilian.

Lilian accepted the voucher to avoid offence. "I'm happy to work with Mr Clarker. I just can't believe he's still here."

"I have tried to fire him. He keeps coming back."

Lilian got up to return to her mountain of work. "I'll give him a call tomorrow. Thanks for the tickets, Dot loves this park."

"How are things at home?" Clarise dropped casually. Lilian appeared exhausted.

Lilian resented defending her husband's unilateral decision. "Fine. William's a surgeon. We're used to him not being around."

Was, Lilian thought.

"You look tired," Clarise said out of concern.

Lilian was aware she was run down.

"Lily's been in hospital with an infection. She's getting better, her nurse caught it early. I'm just a bit of a wreck, I panic every time the phone rings."

"I'm so sorry. Do you need some time off?" Clarise offered.

"Not at the moment." Lilian registered the irony of going to Melbourne to spend time with Lily.

"Did William know Lily was this sick when he left?" Clarise asked judgementally.

No one else had questioned William leaving Lilian when Lily was expected to die at any moment.

"Lily's been dying for a decade," Lilian joked, deflecting for William's sake.

Clarise smiled pityingly, she knew her friend too well. "If you need to go to Melbourne, please just go."

"I suspect I will need to take you up on that offer… soon." Lilian's voice quivered, supressing a sob.

"In the meantime, thanks for taking Mr Clarker," Clarise said, saving her friend from succumbing to her misery with their daughters in the next room.

"No problem." Lilian opened the office door to find Dot thoughtfully sharing her afternoon tea with their colleagues.

Clarise couldn't resist. "Looks like you're doing just fine on your own."

71

"We should watch a movie." Ari was bored.

"No, we're finishing your tax return," Lilian vetoed, one eye on the couch.

"They aren't going to last much longer." Ari waved at their children huddled angelically in front of the television.

"Focus. Tax," Lilian scolded.

"We should have done it before Mum left," Ari sulked.

Lilian laughed. She had been trying to convince Ari to get on top of Carlos' estate well before Dorothy had gone back to Melbourne.

"Have you got the key to the balcony?" Lilian asked.

Ari considered the suspects. "Which one do you think would lock us out here?"

Beth, Lilian thought and went inside to get the key.

"Better safe than sorry. Who would we call? It's two against five," Lilian said, prudently testing the key in the lock.

Ari counted adults on her fingertips. "It used to be one-to-one. We're dropping like flies!"

Connie's fidgeting was beginning to annoy Abbie.

"We could call Dale and Kate? Hold on a sec." Ari went in to separate the twins.

Lilian watched Ari rearrange her daughters and wondered

what it must have been like for Dorothy, widowed with four young children and Lily in a different city.

Ari returned with water.

"You're doing a great job," Lilian commented.

"Thank you. Strangely it got easier when Mum left. I have to get up, there's no one else to feed them."

Lilian had noticed Ari had been in better spirits since Dorothy had moved home.

"Has Mum found a replacement for you at work?" Lilian asked.

"She's still deciding whether to sell or find a new manager. I want her to sell. She deserves a fresh start."

"I agree. Found your passion yet?" Lilian wondered.

Screams emanated from the living room. Ari had jumped out of her seat and reached the door handle before Lilian had even reacted.

Connie had knocked over Abbie's spill-proof bottle and one drop had leaked onto the coffee table. Ari reassured Abbie her drink was fine, and everyone settled down.

"Terrible twos." Ari grumbled. "What were we talking about?"

"What you're going to do for work," Lilian reminded Ari.

Beth had removed herself from the stress of the twins and lay on the rug, too close to the screen. Lilian gestured to her to move back. Beth wriggled on the spot and didn't move an inch.

"I have no idea. I always assumed I would go to uni like you, it just never happened. We got back from travelling and found out I was pregnant with Jordan."

"Do you want a degree?" Lilian said, surprised Ari who had

vehemently hated high school would voluntarily go back into a classroom.

"I'd like a career, so I will probably need a qualification. I want to do something meaningful where I can spend time with people who are nourishing and fun," Ari declared aspirationally.

Lilian was buoyed by her sister's buds of enthusiasm. "I've been thinking about starting a Masters. We can have study sessions together."

"Wow! Where did that come from?" Ari stopped pretending to sort documents.

"Maddison made me realise I'm not growing professionally. I need to push myself, maybe a PhD?"

Ari spung out her chair. "A PhD!"

Jordan frowned, checking through the window whether Ari was jumping for joy or in sadness.

"Sit down, I'm just brainstorming," Lilian quashed the premature celebration. "I've also been thinking about writing a tax history book."

"That's awesome, you should. Or you could do a PhD in tax history?"

"I could." Lilian was intrigued by the fusion.

"Am I right in assuming you haven't discussed any of these ideas with your fugitive husband?"

Lilian laughed, relieved not to have to defend William to her sister. "How can I, he's not here!"

"I hope you aren't putting your life on hold until he gets back, whenever that might be?" Ari couldn't hide her distain. She was furious with William.

"I promise I won't wait once I have decided on a project,"

Lilian guaranteed, not wanting to fuel Ari's grudge.

"What the hell is he doing on the weekends, he could fly home?" Ari digressed, still cross.

There was a crash from inside. They both twisted ready to run, then realised the sound came from the television.

"They're renovating Tom's house. Tom engaged Maggie's interior designer to create one final timeless design in her honour. They've been painting and spending a fortune on furnishings and fixtures."

Amusement diffused Ari's mood. "William is fully aware he's banned from ladders."

Lilian blushed. "Out of sight, out of mind?"

"Well as long as all he gets up to is painting, I guess that's a good thing," Ari suggested cheekily.

Lilian sighed, wishing she had the energy to care what William was up to.

"How are the girls coping?" Ari asked seriously.

"They understand he's with Tom."

"Doesn't sound like it?" Ari commented.

"It's hard to tell, they never complain. There's no love lost, they just don't trust him anymore."

"Does William realise?"

"He calls them every day. He probably thinks that's enough, and that nothing will have changed."

Ari primed to rescue Connie who had fallen asleep and was about to slide off the couch. "Do you think he'd come back if he knew?"

Lilian admired her resilient girls sitting contently with their cousins. "If he did, he'd find they don't adore him like they used to."

72

Ice cream dribbled down Lilian's forearm. William strolled next to her, relaxed, and smiling. So far, the re-enactment was as uncomfortable as the original.

"I can't remember where we were sitting," William admitted, squinting at the row of wooden park benches overlooking the water.

Given it was his idea to recreate their first date, Lilian had presumed he could remember it.

"It was that one," Lilian recalled vividly, as well as her debilitating anxiety, corrosive guilt and the freezing cold.

William sat on the correct bench. Lilian suspected it wouldn't be very romantic to point out that he had been sitting at the other end.

"Happy ten-year anniversary, my love." William toasted with his sundae.

Lilian was begrudgingly touched by the effort. "Happy first date anniversary."

William lifted her sticky hand and kissed it.

"It's interesting you can't remember that date was a disaster?"

"It was not! We held hands and talked all night," William refuted.

Lilian marvelled at his edited remake.

Earlier, when he had picked Lilian up at the terrace, she'd felt resentful William was exploiting her trip to spend time with Lily. As they walked however, Lilian's antipathy had mellowed. She'd forgotten how much she enjoyed her husband's company.

"After that date, I knew we would get married," William declared.

Lilian snorted at the implication she had no free will.

William waited for Lilian to swoon.

Lilian got up and went over to a beach shower and washed the dried ice cream off her arm.

"You're on the wrong side," Lilian succumbed to the truth and William repositioned himself.

"When did you know we'd get married?" William reached for the now clean hand.

Lilian found the question preposterous but played along for the sake of William's nostalgic reincarnation.

"I thought you might be someone I wanted to marry when you gave me the journal for my birthday," Lilian said, remembering their first time surfing together.

"We've had a lot of great dates here in Melbourne."

Lilian's anxiety flared. "Is this where you tell me you're not coming back to Sydney?"

William laughed. "You think I'd end our marriage on our anniversary?"

Lilian stiffened, alarmed.

William realised too late that Lilian was craving reassurance, not comedy. "I'm absolutely coming home. I miss you and I miss the girls, and I miss the surf."

Lilian untensed, annoyed it had taken him so long to say it.

"Sorry, I thought you knew how much I miss you?"

"Really. How would I know that? You're blissfully happy every time we speak," Lilian snapped, feeling rage well and having no desire to tame it.

"I am happy. I'm having a good time with Dad. We've never spent this much time together. Does it have to be one or the other?"

Lilian stood and went to the water fountain and took a long drink, giving her emotions time to settle and accumulate the courage to continue the conversation.

"I'm glad your holiday with Tom is working out the way you'd hoped, but you're missing the point. You wanted us to move back to Melbourne so you could run Tom's clinic," Lilian reminded him.

She wanted to hear he'd ruled out the possibility.

"We've been talking about what to do, whether to sell," William replied awkwardly then trailed off.

Lilian checked a message from Ari.

William stared at the bay.

"I need to head back soon," Lilian said.

She was having lunch with Lily then flying back to collect the girls from Ari so they could sleep in their own beds.

"I'm feeling disorientated without surgery, but I know I don't want to go back. I need to prioritise our family."

Lilian suppressed a laugh. *Leaving is a strange way of prioritising your family*, she thought.

"Do you want to stay in medicine?" Lilian asked, half expecting William had decided to become an interior decorator.

"Definitely. I've been thinking maybe part time medical research or academia or surgical regulation, then I can help manage the Clinic from Sydney. Maybe fly down for the day every couple of weeks for staff meetings."

"If that's what you want." Lilian rejoiced internally, her husband had made some progress toward re-joining their children.

"I'm still not sure. I'm just enjoying being here with Dad, for now," William said, reverting to indecision and inserting a disclaimer.

Mildly reassured, Lilian checked her watch. "Time to go."

She started walking. William stopped her to share a fond glance back at the momentous vista.

"The scene of where it all began," William flirted and leant in dramatically for a kiss.

"I think if you check the record books, you'll find it all began at the Marina." Lilian, done with the charade, ignored his advance.

They walked back to Lily's terrace in silence.

"Do you think you'll be home before Christmas?" Lilian pressed when they had reached the front gate.

Beth and Dot had started asking. It was heartbreaking her daughters were worried their father might have somewhere else to be on Christmas Day.

"I'll be wherever you and the girls are," William responded tactfully.

Lilian felt annoyed by his crafty avoidance of a commitment.

"I asked you if you would be home before Christmas?" Lilian stopped, let go of his hand and turned to look William in the eyes so he wouldn't try avoiding her question a second time.

"I don't know," William admitted sheepishly.

Happy anniversary, she thought.

"Thank you for being honest," Lilian replied coldly and closed the gate. He was not welcome at lunch.

73

"She loved it here," Al said, content to return Lily to her first love.

"She did," Lilian agreed.

Lilian wasn't surprised Lily still planned to be buried with their grandfather. The cemetery gardens had aged alongside Lily, the trees were her familiar friends.

Al steadied himself before negotiating the path with his walking stick.

Dorothy locked the car and walked behind with Ari, both shedding a steady stream of tears.

After the funeral, mourners had gone to the Marina. Once their children were settled, Ari and Lilian had left to accompany Dorothy and Al for their final farewell.

"It was a lovely service. She would have been pleased," Al consoled sweetly.

"I think so." Lilian held his elbow and assisted him to step up onto the grass.

The casket was in place, ready to be lowered into the ground.

Al approached his wife, he laid his hand on the lid, tears dripped onto the pine. He was still wearing his wedding ring. "I will let you say goodbye."

Dorothy appreciated the gesture, thought it wasn't necessary.

Al shuffled back towards the curb.

They stood alongside the hole, Ari and Lilian each with an arm around Dorothy.

"I'm glad I was at home at the end," Dorothy said.

Dorothy had found Lily in the morning. She had passed in her sleep.

Ari took a packet of tissues from her pocket and blew her nose. "I really thought we'd get one last Christmas."

"She was ready," Dorothy assured Ari.

Lily had looked like she'd died a week before her heart had stopped beating.

Lilian's sorrow was tempered by the knowledge Lily had said a proper goodbye to everyone she had loved, with time to spare. Uncharacteristic of departures in their family.

Lilian swivelled to check on Al. An attendant had helped him prop against the trunk of the large tree which shaded Lily's plot.

"I'm so grateful I got to know her. I don't think she realised how much we valued her." Dorothy pulled away from her daughters' embrace to blot her cheeks. "I wish the twins were here."

Marcus and Tim were still on the other side of the world. They'd spent their favours getting back for Lily's birthday party. They'd already said their goodbye.

"Me too," Ari said, also missing her brothers.

Lilian was gaunt, numbed by grief.

"I can't believe we're never going to see her again." Lilian reached out and touched the side of the box, forcing her mind to accept their new reality.

Dorothy exhaled shakily. "Anything anyone wants to say before we do this?"

Lilian and Ari shook their heads. They'd shared their appreciation with Lily while she was alive.

Dorothy signalled they were ready.

Al watched their ceremony from under the tree.

They stood back and contemplated in silence while the attendant began lowering.

Dorothy sobbed, exhausted by the protracted wait for this day.

The casket landed softly on the bottom of the grave.

Ari sprinkled a handful of soil and they left the groundsman to complete the burial.

Lilian went to check on Al.

"I'll see you back at the Marina," Al said, needing more time.

"Are you sure?" Lilian asked, concerned.

"I'm fine, dear. I would like to stay for a while," Al assured her. "I'll call a taxi."

Lilian felt uncomfortable leaving Al alone in the hot sun. "Mind if I join you?"

"Please do," Al replied sombrely and tucked his soaked handkerchief into his pocket.

Lilian followed Ari and Dorothy to collect her bag.

"I'm so grateful we got to see how happy Mum was when she fell in love with Al," Dorothy said.

Lilian remembered the shock of Lily's engagement announcement. "They really were perfect for each other."

"We couldn't have asked for a better step-grandfather," Ari agreed.

At the car, Lilian hugged Dorothy. "See you later."

Lilian messaged William to let him know she would meet

them back at Tom's, then walked back to the tree.

She attempted to sit gracefully.

"Your eulogy was beautiful. I liked the anecdote about your breakfasts together in the courtyard. I didn't realise you had lived at the terrace for so long."

"Yes, high school and university. Lily practically raised me. I would be a very different person if it wasn't for her," Lilian reminisced. Lily had supplemented Dorothy over those years.

"How so?" Al asked, happy to sit on the grass and hear about Lily for the rest of the afternoon.

A stiff breeze lashed the tree, and several leaves fell upon Lily's grave.

"I was easily overwhelmed. Lily was determined to enjoy every day. She instilled in me not to be defined by events out of my control, to be my own person."

Al smiled at the traits he had admired in his late wife.

"I hope she knew how much I loved her." Lilian succumbed to warm grief-full tears.

Al patted her hand. "She knew."

74

Lilian inspected her blazer in the reflection of the meeting room window. Her outfit had survived the flight and the taxi, and she appeared fresher than she felt.

Walking through the entrance to the Tax Office headquarters, Lilian had been surprised that the lobby hadn't changed. She had signed in as a visitor. A worker she didn't know had ushered Lilian inside and offered her a latte. Then a different stranger had delivered the drink. Lilian felt peculiar to be foreign in a place she knew so well.

"Sorry I kept you waiting," Henrietta apologised as she dashed in, coffee mug in hand. "It's so good to see you."

"Likewise."

Henrietta wrapped one arm around Lilian and hugged hard.

"It's been chaos here today. There's been a change to income tax rates for small business and half the systems have crashed. IT can't figure out why, so we've had to pause all our processing until they can figure out what's wrong."

Lilian was tickled by nerves from waiting to explain why she had requested the meeting.

"How's William, and the family?"

"Well thanks. Lily passed away recently so everyone's a bit flat," Lilian answered. She didn't want to divulge the state of her marriage.

"I'm so sorry. That's awful. Was she sick?"

Henrietta had been one of Lilian's closest confidants, but they hadn't managed to keep in touch after Lilian left Canberra.

"No, just old age," Lilian offered minimally. "How are you?"

"Busy here, family's well, not much to report," Henrietta replied curtly. "You look great by the way. What are you doing in Canberra?"

Lilian wondered whether Henrietta was also omitting an uncomfortable truth. "I came to see you."

"You're only in Canberra to see me? You could have just called," Henrietta said, embarrassed.

"Actually, I wanted to see how it felt being back here. I've been thinking about returning to the Tax Office," Lilian explained, aware she was blindsiding her former boss. Lilian wanted to see Henrietta's real reaction, not listen to a rehearsed answer.

Henrietta lent back in her chair and examined Lilian thoughtfully. "Is this a roundabout way of asking me for a job?"

Lilian smiled. Henrietta's healthy scepticism had served her well while she pulled herself up the ranks.

"No, well not in Canberra. If I was going to come back, I would need to work from Sydney."

"I had a feeling I was going to hear from you. Maddison told me you rejected an obscene amount of money to manage her company because you love tax." Henrietta laughed, relieved she wasn't being trounced.

Someone tapped on the door of the meeting room to sneak Henrietta an urgent message.

"Sorry about that."

"No problem, I forgot you're friends with Maddison." Lilian was amazed Maddison would be so indelicate so as to reveal private details of a business negotiation.

"Yes, she was upset that you turned her down."

Lilian felt annoyed, she hadn't flown from another city to talk about Maddison.

"Before I approach the Sydney branch, I was wanting to ask you whether anything major has changed?" Lilian asked frankly, hoping for something insightful.

Henrietta's expression revealed her thoughts.

"From memory, you weren't very happy when you left. Why do you want to come back?"

"I struggled with the politics, but I always loved the work. I have a different perspective now I've had experience on the outside."

Working with Maddison had reminded her what it felt like to make a difference.

A colleague thumped on the window, the room was required for the next meeting.

"I'd definitely have you back, I'm sure we could work something out," Henrietta replied hopefully, heartened by Lilian's response.

"I wouldn't be able to come back to Canberra, but remote might work." Flying to Canberra while William was intermittently returning to Melbourne would be a nightmare.

Henrietta collected her mug. As soon as she opened the door, they were stampeded by a dozen associates clamouring to get the best seat.

Henrietta's phone buzzed repeatedly. She was required elsewhere. "Do you want to meet the team?"

"Sorry, I have to get back to the airport."

"Let me walk you out," Henrietta said, too busy to argue.

Staff sped frantically past them in the corridors.

"I didn't answer your question. Other than the new faces, nothing really changes around here. If you left because of office politics, if anything, it's worse," Henrietta admitted, hoping not to frighten Lilian away.

Lilian assumed as much. Her tax friends still gossiped about their dealings with the public service.

They arrived at the entrance lobby and Lilian embraced Henrietta.

"I appreciate you making time for me today," Lilian said, remorseful for ambushing her old friend.

"I'm glad you came, and I'm sorry I didn't have more time, or better advice. I'll be in touch if I hear of anything in Sydney," Henrietta assured her, impressed by Lilian's assertiveness.

Henrietta rushed back inside, and Lilian called a taxi. The Tax Office may not have changed, but she had.

75

Jamie had proposed they meet during his lunch break. He was in Sydney for a business conference.

On paper it was a platonic well-lit lunch between friends at an appropriately corporate restaurant. But the second Jamie sat down, Lilian discovered the spark between them hadn't faded.

They had eaten and chatted easily about work. Other than a few handsome creases at the corners of his eyes, Jamie hadn't aged a day.

"I can't believe you have four kids," Lilian said. "I'm maxed out with two."

"You are one of four kids," Jamie teased.

"I know, my poor mother." Lilian laughed in spite of herself.

"My wife wanted four, so we had four."

Lilian bit her tongue, Jamie had told her he wanted four children.

"You don't want more?" Jamie added.

Lilian was thrown by the question. Jamie noticed her hesitate over the answer.

"Sorry, too personal. It just feels like, no time has passed." Jamie blushed.

Lilian coloured brighter in reply and changed the subject.

"How did you meet your wife," she asked, safely.

"Courtney and I started at the firm together as graduates. Now we're both partners. We don't fight unless it's about contract law." Jamie laughed.

Lilian suspected that one liner was normally used to charm clients.

"What about you? William, was it?"

"William and I met at the Marina. We used to work together," Lilian replied unashamedly.

Jamie didn't comment on the timing.

"Is he a sailor?"

Lilian laughed. "William can sail, but no, he's, was a surgeon."

"That's handy. We practically live at the medical centre. At least one of our kids is broken most of the time," Jamie joked. "William is or was a surgeon?"

Lilian pondered whether a career change was a private marital matter.

"William is thinking about taking over his father's general practice clinic. Personally, I think he'll end up going back to surgery. He's so talented, it would be an enormous loss to the profession."

The waiter arrived with the bill but Jamie ordered another coffee.

He frowned, quickly connecting the dots. "Is that in Melbourne?"

Lilian had been avoiding mentioning William's absence, but she'd led Jamie straight to the fact.

"It is. William's in Melbourne at the moment while he figures out what he wants to do next."

Jamie didn't appear to find the arrangement unusual.

"What made you fall in love with him?" Jamie asked, his smile bordering on salacious.

Lilian was momentarily startled by the question, then she realised Jamie was curious because he was jealous. She took a sip of water and exaggerated thinking about the answer.

"I fell in love with William because he was so thoughtful. He pays attention to what matters to me, and he listens. Fortunately, he's also gorgeous," Lilian gushed, satisfied her disclosure was sufficiently adoring to deter Jamie acting on any remnant feelings. "What about you and your wife?"

"Courtney and I have a lot in common. We run together, work together, do everything together pretty much."

"Sounds like you found your soulmate," Lilian remarked, glad Jamie had received the message that she wasn't interested.

Jamie nodded.

They sat in an awkward silence, Jamie processing Lilian's subtle rejection.

"I couldn't believe it when I ran into Rachel and she told me you two had written a book," Jamie said, desperate to orient the conversation away from their spouses.

"Rachel wrote most of it, but we had a lot of fun. She's been trying to rope me in to writing another together." Lilian laughed, relieved Jamie had regained his composure.

"You don't want to?"

Lilian contemplated giving the honest answer.

"I haven't thought about it. Lily died recently, our whole family has been on pause for a while."

"I'm sorry to hear that. Why are you on pause?" Jamie asked, not understanding the correlation.

"We didn't know when we would have to fly to Melbourne to take care of her, or arrange healthcare, or say goodbye or plan the funeral. None of us committed to anything for ages," Lilian said. She had been living in limbo.

Jamie's cappuccino arrived.

"Makes sense. I haven't lost anyone from that generation yet, touch wood, and we all live in the same suburb." Jamie laughed and rubbed the wooden table to ensure he retained his good fortune.

How boring, Lilian thought.

"So now Lily's gone, do you want to write a book with Rachel?" Jamie added, returning to benign territory.

Lilian was irritated by the question. She wanted to be having this conversation with her husband. She wanted to be at home with her husband cooking her lunch in their kitchen, not out at a pretentious restaurant with a mis-intentioned ex.

"I'm considering writing a history of tax policy," Lilian responded while glancing at her watch.

Jamie grinned. "Still obsessed with tax."

"Completely obsessed. I'm fortunate to have found a career I love," Lilian said flatly.

"New book, perfect husband, great job, sounds like you've got it all?" Jamie teased.

Lilian gestured to the waiter to bring the bill. "For now."

76

"The school called the office because I was in a meeting and didn't answer my phone. So Jason panicked and called William who told Jason to take Dot to our local doctor," Lilian fumed.

"Oh no. Was Dot all right?" Rachel asked.

Lilian changed from the blue suit dress to the grey.

"Dot was fine, she loves Jason, but he now has the cold he caught from Dot and hasn't been at work all week," Lilian ranted, inspecting herself in the mirror.

"Why are you so angry?" Rachel said nervously.

"So many reasons, Rachel. So many! I'm angry my husband had the audacity to tell my boss to pick up his child from school. I'm angry my husband isn't here to pick up his own child, and I'm angry my children are being ferried around like they're being raised in a commune!"

Rachel laughed. "I'm sorry. I know you're upset. I'm trying to be supportive, but it's very funny."

Lilian managed a smile at the sight of Rachel sniggering in the corner of the dressing room.

"It's not funny," Lilian disagreed goodhumoredly.

"To play devil's advocate, you're going to an interview you haven't told William about, and you went on a date with your ex, so I guess, maybe it all evens out in the end," Rachel noted cheekily.

"You make me sound like the villain. There's only one villain in this story and he's in Melbourne pretending he's an interior decorator!" Lilian scolded Rachel playfully but accepted her loyal friend's critique in jest.

Lilian took off the grey suit and left the icky brown two-piece on its hanger.

"Which one did you like? I liked the blue?" Lilian asked.

Rachel sighed, spent from laughing.

"The blue was the best." Rachel peeled herself off the carpet to help place garments back on their hangers. "Have you asked William to come home?"

"No. I don't want him back if he's not ready," Lilian said, rejecting the assertion she was to blame for her husband's absence.

"Do you want him to come home?" Rachel rephrased.

"I do, but, I just hope it's soon," Lilian said cryptically.

Rachel opened the door and poked her head out. There was no one listing to their conversation.

Lilian went to find the cashier.

Rachel left the store in search of eateries.

Lilian paid then waited outside on the pavement for Rachel to return.

"Sorry I got distracted by wedding dresses. This way," Rachel apologised, and they started walking to the café she'd discovered tucked in an arcade.

"I didn't go on a date with Jamie, we just had lunch," Lilian corrected.

Rachel laughed. "Yeah, a lunch date."

"If anything, it reminded me how much I do love William," Lilian replied, defensively.

"That's sweet, but it doesn't change the fact that you're planning to change jobs and you don't want to talk to him about it." Rachel was surprised Lilian was being so reckless with her marriage.

Lilian wanted to argue with Rachel, but she was right.

"It's not that I don't want to talk to him about it. I can't trust that if I ask him what he thinks about me changing jobs he won't give me biased answer based on what he wants."

Rachel saw the anguish flash across Lilian's face and pulled her to a stop outside the café to address her statement with the gravity it required.

"I've never heard you speak like this. Do you really believe that?" Rachel asked sadly.

Lilian wished she could look away and deny it, but it was the painful truth. Lilian's comment was harsh but fair.

"Yes, I do." Lilian broke away from Rachel's stare.

Rachel went inside and ordered takeaway sandwiches and they waited in the lane.

"Beginning of the end?" Rachel said, not convinced by Lilian's earlier response.

Lilian sighed. She believed what she had told Jamie, she was still in love with William.

"No, just the beginning of something different. If I want my marriage to work, I have to stand up for myself. As my mother would say, stop being naive."

Rachel smiled, comforted and a little impressed. "So mature."

"We've talked about me all day. How are you?" Lilian asked, aware she needed to collect Beth from kindergarten.

"That's because your life's more interesting than mine.

Wedding planning is going well. Research is going well."

"I'm glad you started writing without me. What's this book about?"

"Superannuation strategies. People realise super wasn't designed to cover all retirement expenses then write to me and ask me what they should do. I could already fill an entire book with all my past responses," Rachel said, testing her elevator pitch on Lilian.

"That's a great idea, I can't wait to read it," Lilian praised, excited.

"I'd love you to write a chapter on tax implications. Early withdrawals, salary sacrificing, that kind of thing?" Rachel sowed the seed.

The server came over with their sandwiches. Lilian needed to leave.

"Sure, but you'll have to babysit while I'm working. I'm a single parent," Lilian joked.

"Or I could convince your husband to come home and take care of his children?" Rachel teased.

Lilian laughed. "Good luck!"

77

Dorothy unfolded two camp chairs and pulled champagne and plastic cups from a shopping bag. She lay a stack of tissues under the bottle to prevent condensation from spoiling her new vintage floorboards.

"The view is breathtaking. I can see why you bought it." Lilian ran her pointer finger over the inbuilt curved art deco shelving in the corner of the room. "Juan didn't mind?"

Dorothy admired her living room. "We looked at it together but it's too small for both of us. I told him I needed some time before I move in with him. The place we bought to live in after the wedding is a new build, its much bigger."

Lilian went to explore the bedrooms. She opened all the cupboards and drawers, inspecting the intricate detailing.

Lilian joined Dorothy back in the living room. "The tiling in the bathroom is beautiful."

"I love everything about every room. It felt like home the second I stepped through the door," Dorothy replied, pouring the champagne.

Lilian hesitated, not wanting to spoil the celebratory mood.

"Why do you want your own apartment?" Lilian asked, taking the sweating bottle and placing it in the sink.

"I just feel more comfortable having my own place,

particularly for when the twins come back. You never know what might happen in the future."

Lilian laughed. "I wouldn't be letting those grubs anywhere near this apartment."

Dorothy smiled, the thought had crossed her mind.

"Well, wherever you decide to live, I'm glad we'll be in Sydney together. You moved back to Melbourne straight after our wedding. We've not lived in the same city since I was a teenager."

"Me too, it doesn't feel like it."

Dorothy got up to lower a blind, the sun was dazzling off the harbour.

"Do you want to talk about the terrace?" Lilian asked.

"Sure."

Lily had left the terrace to Dorothy and Lilian in equal share. They hadn't been alone to discuss the bequest since Al had given them a copy of Lily's will.

"Lily never told me what she expected us to do with it. Did she tell you?"

Dorothy sipped her champagne and embraced the sadness which reappeared whenever she thought of her mother.

"She didn't. I assumed she would leave it to you."

Lilian was surprised. "I wonder whether she left it to both of us so we'd be less likely to sell. Keep the terrace for future generations?"

Dorothy was touched by the depths of Lilian's sentiment. "Mum wasn't that calculated."

Lilian was hoping to be able to fall back on Lily's wishes and avoid the confronting decision.

They sat, thinking, taking in the view.

"I would like to sell. But if you want to keep the terrace for the family, I'm fine with that," Dorothy said, hoping to alleviate Lilian's paralysis.

"I can't imagine anyone using it, now we're all in Sydney," Lilian supposed.

"What did William think?" Dorothy asked warily. Lilian appeared to have discounted William's family.

"He thinks we should do whatever Lily wanted us to do."

"It's up to you, there's no hurry. I'm home for good but I could see you going back to live in Melbourne," Dorothy alluded.

"Really?"

Lilian was a little offended that, even after her protracted battle with William to keep her children in Sydney, Dorothy thought Lilian might cave.

"I think you've forgotten that you loved living in Melbourne and William loved growing up in Melbourne. Of course you want to be near family while the girls are young but once they've grown up, you two might want to go back."

If we make it that far, Lilian thought.

Lilian hadn't considered what she might want at Dorothy's age.

"Or the girls may want to follow in your footsteps and study in Melbourne," Dorothy added.

Lilian laughed. "You are posing a lot of hypotheticals."

Beth was getting cheekier by the day. Lilian could absolutely envisage her youngest running off to Melbourne.

Lilian sighed. "It's the rational decision to sell, but it feels very, final. Saying goodbye to Lily was hard enough, selling the terrace is like saying goodbye to Melbourne as well."

Dorothy was struck by the statement. Her brilliant daughter could always synthesise the complexity of a situation and distil it eloquently into a handful of words.

"In that case, let's rent it out and sell when you're sure," Dorothy recommended, mindful William may have other ideas.

A boat horn echoed through the empty apartment.

"Sounds good." Tears stung Lilian's eyes. It was horridly painful to imagine anyone but Lily sitting in their courtyard. "I wish I'd asked her what she wanted."

Dorothy smiled. "She wanted you to be happy."

78

"Happy Birthday, Mummy!" Beth squealed and handed over her gift.

Lilian's colleagues applauded.

"This is the most beautiful drawing of a cat and a dolphin that I have ever seen," Lilian said while hugging Beth, who was perched on the edge of her desk.

Next Dot presented Lilian with a store wrapped present.

Who took her to buy this, Lilian thought.

Lilian ripped the paper and found a calendar for next year with black and white photos of Bondi.

"This is excellent, Dot. Thank you." Lilian kissed her cheek.

"Auntie Ari helped me," Dot blurted, desperate to be rid of the secret.

"That was very nice of her," Lilian commented, mindful her children were yet again distracting the entire office.

Unexpectedly, Jason appeared with a cake. Beth and Dot initiated a chorus of Happy Birthday.

"Gluten free, dairy free, egg free, vegan and no candles," Jason announced, accounting for all sensitivities. The local bakery was kindly accommodating.

"I think its carob and orange," Jason whispered to Lilian then directed his staff back to their desks.

Lilian began to cut up her cake.

"Do you want to wait for Daddy in the kitchen," Lilian prompted.

"I'll wait here," Beth yelled excitedly.

"We have to go to the kitchen, Mum needs to do work now," Dot interpreted for Beth.

Lilian smiled proudly at Dot's gentle sistering and handed them both chunky slices on serviettes, certain neither would eat it.

Dot took Beth's hand and led her away.

"He won't be long," Lilian called.

She finished distributing the cake and went to give a piece to Jason and Clarise.

Clarise was scowling at her computer when Lilian knocked, the door was open. "Can I come in?"

"Sure. Can you close the door please. I can't concentrate with Yael and Mala constantly bickering," Clarise complained.

Lilian entered and closed the door, placing the cake on the desk.

"I'm not eating that cardboard," Clarise replied.

Lilian laughed. "Thanks for having Beth in the office today. She's been jealous because Dot gets to spend afternoons with me."

"That's alright, everyone loves your kids. Beth is adorable," Clarise answered. It was high praise, their colleagues were easily agitated.

Guilt-ridden for insulting their baker, Clarise tasted the cake.

"Thank you. It won't be for too much longer," Lilian assured her.

"Has William decided to steal your daughters and take them to Melbourne?"

Lilian disregarded the dig.

"I wanted to ask you if you would be a referee for me. I've been offered a job," Lilian revealed.

"Congratulations," Clarise smiled genuinely. "Obviously that's awful news for me but that's great for you!"

Lilian laughed at Clarise's bluntness. It really was awful news for Bondi Singh, Lilian was custodian of their most challenging clients.

"It's not a done deal. They need to complete the reference check before they can offer me the role officially," Lilian cautioned.

"No pressure," Clarise joked. She didn't have a bad word to say about Lilian. "Of course, please give them my personal number."

"Thanks, don't give away my job yet."

"I don't even want to think about you leaving. Jason will be happy."

"What! Why?"

"He doesn't like being your boss." Clarise looked at Lilian pityingly, she was blind to her own appeal. Jason didn't like green tea.

Lilian was baffled by the comment and Clarise kindly changed the subject.

"I have a birthday present for you." Clarise pulled the package from her top draw.

"That's not necessary," Lilian said. Clarise's generous flexibility was gift enough.

Lilian unwrapped the box. It contained a rare tax textbook

from the early twentieth century.

"Thank you! I have been trying to find a copy of this for ages." Lilian jumped out of her chair and traversed the desk to hug Clarise.

"It's no cat and dolphin," Clarise joked.

Lilian laughed. "This is perfect."

"I thought it would provide inspiration for your book," Clarise mumbled, embarrassed by the affection. "What did you get from William?"

"Nothing yet," Lilian replied. "He's on his way from the airport now."

"He didn't come back for your birthday?" Clarise commented, shocked.

"He had to be at home for a furniture delivery this morning."

"Home?" Clarise queried with a raised eyebrow.

"Sorry, I meant Tom's house," Lilian corrected, blushing.

"Someone needs to slap him. He needs to get his priorities straight," Clarise declared angrily.

Lilian realised she was supposed to be mad and felt ashamed that she was just relieved her husband was coming home at all.

"It's fine," Lilian placated Clarise. "I was planning on working today anyway. Honestly, it's totally fine."

"What are you guys doing tonight?"

"We're going out to dinner with my family. It should be a fun night."

Beth opened the door without knocking.

"Can I have more cake?" she asked.

"Sure, here." Lilian passed Beth the slice she was going to give Jason, now warm from sitting in her hand.

Clarise was still scowling when Beth closed the door.

"I'm amazed she ate that cake." Lilian laughed.

"Is William back for good?" Clarise probed, not finished with her inquiry.

"No, just for the weekend."

Clarise pursed her lips, unable to contain her disgust. "How long are going to put up with this?"

Lilian was taken aback by her friend's temper, but she knew Clarise's frustration was born of concern. It wasn't just Lilian affected by William's holiday.

Lilian was tired of parenting alone. "Not long."

79

William passed the photograph to Lilian and placed its empty frame in the moving box.

Lilian read Lily's anecdote on the back. Lily had recorded the date and noted Dorothy had enjoyed her tenth birthday party.

"I never knew Lily had written on the back of all these photos," Lilian commented, amazed.

William smiled then collected the next memory from the wall and unclasped the backboard.

Lilian affixed the photo to the album, then copied the message onto the page.

They had archived about a fifth of the photos in the hallway.

"What do you want to do with the frames?" William asked.

"Op shop."

As directed, William taped up the full box and took it to the car with the rest of the trinkets to be donated.

Lilian went to the wall, dislodged the next photograph, and opened the frame. She read the caption. A summer holiday with Eric, Dorothy, Lilian, and Ari, before the twins were born. The photo was small, square, and grainy. One of the few containing Lilian and her father.

Lilian placed the photo back in the frame, replaced the glass and added it to a box to take back to Sydney.

"Mum, look what I found," Dot yelled from the library.

Beth and Dot were helping Dorothy pack the books going to the second-hand book shop. Lilian had already inspected the shelves and saved what she wanted to keep.

On her way down the hall Lilian admired the patchwork of preserved wallpaper hidden by the frames, an imprint of Lily's long life.

Dot held a dainty lace bookmark with a tassel she'd found pressed between the pages. "Can I keep it?"

"If you'd like." Lilian reached out her hand. "I'll put it with the other things we're taking home."

Dot handed over the bookmark and got back to work.

Beth flipped through one of Lily's fashion chronicles, admiring the dresses. Dorothy and Lilian shared a smile over Beth's obliviousness, then she went back to continue preserving their history.

She placed the bookmark on top of the photograph of her father and thought ahead to the kitchen.

William returned with an empty box and selected the next frame from the wall.

"Jane called last night. She wants Lily's cocktail shaker," Lilian remembered.

"Happy memories?"

"Jane liked to party with Lily's friends," Lilian explained, recalling the late nights and messy mornings.

"What furniture do you want to keep?" William asked. They'd only just started. The hallway needed to be cleared before they could remove the furnishings.

Lilian considered what was left in the house after Dorothy's ruthless decluttering.

"I would like to keep the table and chairs from the courtyard." Lilian gestured to the tired set, rusted from the rain and years of waiting to be needed.

"It would look good in our garden," William agreed awkwardly.

Lilian scoured the living room. They didn't need anything. The only thing in the room she wanted was William.

"I don't think we'll be able to rent it out in this condition. We'll have to get it painted and new carpets," Lilian remarked.

"I can arrange everything while I'm down here," William offered.

"I would rather you came home," Lilian responded sharply and put the album on the table.

William flinched at the directness. "Can we talk about this later when the girls aren't here?"

Lilian put her on hand on her hip, ignoring his request. "You know, our friends can't believe you're still here. I appreciate you're spending time with Tom, but no one else can understand why you haven't come home yet."

"We're not finished the renovations," William replied matter-of-factly, accepting Lilian wasn't heeding his request for a postponement.

"That's what I mean. William, our friends can't believe you would rather be in Melbourne completing a renovation than in Sydney with your wife and children," Lilian reiterated pointedly.

Defenceless, William turned back to prying a frame.

"I'm starting to wonder the same thing."

William looked up and contemplated his response. He'd opened his mouth to speak when Beth stepped into the living room with her new favourite book under her arm.

"I'm hungry," Beth announced.

"That's because it's almost dinner time. Do you want Dad to take you down to the Marina for some chips?"

Beth nodded and snuggled into Lilian, worn out by the adventure.

"Can you take them for dinner, and I'll meet you back at Tom's," Lilian instructed.

Defeated, William looked around for his keys and wallet that were sitting on the kitchen bench. He smiled meekly and lifted Beth onto his shoulders. "Let's go get you some chips."

William collected Dot from the library and left.

Lilian continued archiving the photos.

Dorothy popped her head into the living room. "He didn't look very happy, is everything alright?"

"I suspect my husband has just realised he's pushed his luck a bit too far," Lilian replied mysteriously.

"Are you alright?" Dorothy frowned.

Lilian smiled. "I'm great."

80

Beth drenched Connie in sunscreen. Dot covered Abbie evenly, then saved Connie from Beth.

"Not too bad. They'd be fine without us," Ari joked once her twins were sufficiently protected from the sun.

"Not funny." Lilian laughed hollowly, still raw from compounding loss.

Jordan paddled in the rockpools, collecting water for the moat he'd dug around Dot's sandcastle.

"Here's to the new matriarch of the family." Ari raised her water bottle to toast Dorothy.

"No, thank you. That makes me sound ancient," Dorothy said, rejecting the title.

"You don't have a choice, Grandma," Ari teased.

"Fine, I'll hold the mantel for now, as long as I'm not compared to Lily."

Lilian watched Beth creep toward the ocean, torn between fear and curiosity.

"Seriously though, thank you for taking care of me. I wouldn't have survived without you both," Ari acknowledged sentimentally.

Dot went to steer Beth away from the waves. Relieved, Beth joined the twins making casts of shells with wet sand.

"You don't need to thank me. I need to thank you. I don't know what I would have done when William left if you both weren't around to help with the girls."

"You're welcome," Dorothy said, remembering fondly her years nursing Lily. "I'm sure you will have an opportunity to repay the favour."

"Lucky for us you're back in Sydney so we'll be able to take care of you here when you get old," Ari said happily and raised her water bottle again. "Here's to Melbourne. May it rest in peace, once William is back in Sydney obviously."

Lilian laughed at Ari's theatrics. Dorothy frowned at being the next in line for homecare.

"Speaking of Melbourne, Al mailed me a painting Lily made while she was staying with him at the retirement village. Did you know she painted? It's excellent, I'm having it framed," Lilian said, reminded of the people she missed down south.

"I had no idea, but it's nice you're still in touch with Al," Dorothy said.

"She was so talented and secretive," Ari mused. While emptying the terrace they had discovered countless achievements and interests they had never known about while Lily was alive.

"I think you mean modest," Dorothy corrected.

Beth returned for a cuddle and a packet of sultanas and then skipped away gleefully.

"I'm not sure what I should be more upset about, that my husband won't come home or that my children are completely fine without him," Lilian wondered aloud.

"Are you upset though?" Dorothy asked.

"I don't have time to be upset but I wish I was."

"What's there to be upset about? You've got an awesome new job and you're writing a book," Ari joked.

"You sound like Rachel," Lilian claimed.

"Where are you going to put him when he gets back?" Ari teased.

"I'm sure we'll find room for him somewhere." Lilian laughed, feeling sorry for William.

Ari went to play with the twins who'd grown bored with moulding sand.

"The water's beautiful, are you going in?" Dorothy encouraged.

"Maybe later," Lilian replied, content to lie in the sun and oversee her daughters playing.

Dorothy rested peacefully on her lounge.

"Why did you fall in love with Juan?" Lilian asked.

Dorothy lifted the sunhat off her face. "Where did that come from?"

"An old friend asked me why I fell in love with William. I have been wondering whether it even matters why we fell in love in the first place?"

Dorothy considered her first and last loves. "I fell in love with Juan because he's loyal, intelligent, respectful and patient."

Lilian smiled, qualities she also loved in her own husband.

"What did you tell your friend?"

"I said I fell in love with William because he's thoughtful, a good listener, and pays attention. But he can't be any of those things when he's not around," Lilian noted sadly.

"Perhaps a decade later you don't stay together for the same reasons. But if you can remember why you fell in love, at least you have something to hold on to when things get hard,"

Dorothy said, recalling the challenging times with Eric.

"If William doesn't come back to Sydney, the girls and I will be fine. What scares me is if he comes home, and we don't love each other anymore."

"What matters is, you still want to try," Dorothy offered kindly.

Dorothy's sunhat blew off and went spinning down the beach. She jumped up and chased after it as it tumbled towards to water. Dot and Jordan ran after her to help. Jordan caught up with the hat just before it landed in the ocean.

Dorothy stayed at the edge of the waves to play with her grandchildren, holding them protectively as they dipped their toes in the water.

Ari came back to lie next to Lilian on her blistering towel.

"Today is perfect, all of us together," Ari said.

But they weren't all together. Between loss and distance, Lilian knew her heart would always be in pieces.

Warm from love and sunshine, she relaxed into the beach chair and smiled. "Feels like perfect."

Other Titles from Emma Adair

2068
The Mace Mystery and Other Musings

www.ingramcontent.com/pod-product-compliance
Lightning Source LLC
Chambersburg PA
CBHW022032290426
44109CB00014B/832